RICHMOND
MURDER & MAYHEM

RICHMOND
MURDER & MAYHEM

SELDEN RICHARDSON

THE
History
PRESS

Published by The History Press
Charleston, SC
www.historypress.com

Copyright © 2023 by Selden Richardson
All rights reserved

Cover photos from the archives of the Richmond Times-Dispatch, *used with permission.*

First published 2023

Manufactured in the United States

ISBN 9781467151634

Library of Congress Control Number: 2022951597

This book is dedicated to the memory of my good friend Wyatt S. Richardson, whose guiding paw was sorely missed when this project began.

CONTENTS

PREFACE

Perhaps it is a form of self-preservation that we imagine the world we live in is the ultimate of human experiences and historic events, even if our own memories are some imperfectly formed and sepia-toned reality that is no longer with us. We don't want reminders that one day we, too, will be overtaken by that same blanketing fog of history. The concept that things so real, so vivid, so alive for us now could one day be consigned to that hazy space seems impossible.

In Richmond, as everywhere, the historian's task is to breach that haze, animate the past and let it speak to us, while at the same time re-creating that distant world. A young Italian immigrant who has been dead for eighty years, with a little imagination, can be glimpsed watching traffic from behind a Broad Street display window. An otherwise undistinguished Grove Avenue doorway swings open today as it did in 1927, and a man rushes out carrying a woman in his arms. A quiet patch of piney woods conceals where an airplane full of young men fell from the sky. We share these spaces with these people of the past, and only the membrane of time makes them seem so inaccessible.

My most vivid experience when the fog called "today" parted for a moment occurred, improbably, in a Starbucks at Richmond's River Road Shopping Center. I was nursing a cup of coffee and writing about a doomed couple who had, in the course of the wife's last afternoon, walked west together down what is now Huguenot Road on a route that took them past where I was sitting. Looking over the lid of my laptop, I felt the hair on the back of my neck move. There they were on the other side of the road from me, and just for a second, the plate glass window and the traffic all dropped away and silence descended. He was wearing an army-issue trench coat, she was wearing a borrowed man's overcoat and I could see they were chatting as they walked. They were *just there*, as real as the people in that Starbucks, but all I could do was mutely watch them from across the street, even though I knew he would murder her within minutes.

The past had risen just below the surface like a koi in a pond, showed its form and rich color for just a second and then sank again into the dark. I shook my head and looked around the café, hoping that my mouth hadn't been open the whole time I was daydreaming. My coffee was getting cold, but I didn't care because I had felt the full force and certainty of what Mr. Faulkner famously assured us: the past is ever with us.

The reader will note that the paths of many of these stories often lead to one of Richmond's cemeteries, where the subject of the account can often be found. From humble stone to grand grave markers, or even a featureless expanse of grass, the dead make their final plea to be remembered: *I was here in this place. I lived and loved and I died on this day, and I was real.* Hopefully, these accounts assist that declaration, give voice to those lives and illuminate some of the lesser-known events that make up this city's long and often colorful story.

ACKNOWLEDGEMENTS

F irst and foremost, I'd like to thank my wife, Karri, and our daughter, Lelia, for their love and patience while I spent so much time "booking," as we all grew to call my solitary task. I'd also like to thank Ray Bonis, editor of the *Shockoe Examiner*, for his encouragement and help, as some of these stories appeared in that Richmond history blog in shorter versions. Staff of the *Richmond Times-Dispatch* gave valuable assistance with photographs from one of Richmond's great unsung resources: the newspaper's photograph archive. The descendants of Patrolman John A. Tibbs were very generous in speaking with me about his murder, and thanks also to the Richmond Police Department for even a limited look at its files. Rex Poole very kindly shared his childhood memories of the tragedy that took his father's life in the horrific crash of Imperial Airlines Flight 201/8. Other people who helped make this book possible were the staff of the Library of Virginia, The Valentine and the Presbyterian Cemetery in Lynchburg.

Chapter 1

MEDICINAL MURDER

A YOUNG GROOM SIMPLIFIES HIS LIFE WITH CYANIDE

Alice Knight smiles out of her photograph, taken in 1918. Her hair is curly and dark, her face full and round and her smile lopsided and bucktoothed, with a gap between her upper front teeth. Her look seems to signal a sense of humor and a hearty, sincere laugh, and she appears to be the kind of girl who might prefer a mug of beer to a sip of sherry. It is her eyes, however, that still shine through the dim pane of time: perhaps blue, light-colored, alert and cheerful. She grins at the camera, a new bride with her entire life suddenly broadening and unfolding, full of promise and affection. But Alice's life had hardly begun when it was over, murdered by the new husband who was supposed to love and protect her. According to her death certificate, Alice's life lasted exactly nineteen years, six months and seven days.[1]

A photograph of Alice's new husband, Lemuel Johnson, from the same period is very different. Taken from the 1917 Medical College of Virginia student yearbook (the year of his graduation from dental school), Lemuel hardly looks celebratory. Behind his spectacles, his eyes appear pained, and his downturned mouth is hardly the confident look of a young man ready to make his way in the world. Lemuel had good reason to look unhappy, even though he had passed the North Carolina Dental Board exams and was ready to return to his native state and establish his practice.[2]

The United States entered World War I in April 1917, just as Lemuel was finishing his medical education. He was one of thousands of men who received notification that they might be called up for enlistment as the country prepared to go to war. The prospect of being sent to France worried Lemuel, as it would spoil his plans, never mind the threat of being killed or wounded in action. In addition, both his parents were unwell, and trying to provide for them would be impossible if the army had him in its grasp. There was also a slight problem with his marriage.

Lemuel met Alice Knight in Richmond at the School of Dentistry, where she was a stenographer. They soon fell in love and were secretly married on September 18, 1917.[3] Lemuel broached the subject of marriage with Alice's mother weeks before, jokingly asking, "Do you mind my making a Tarheel out of Alice?" but the girl's parents had no idea of the event until they were shown the marriage license.[4] Lemuel told Alice that he wanted to keep their marriage secret. "He said that the reason was that his father wanted him to marry an old maid schoolteacher in North Carolina," and he needed some time to break the news to his parents. He would later blame the secrecy on Alice, but her friends called that a lie.[5]

The real problem was that in Lemuel's hometown, Miss Ollie White proudly wore the engagement ring he had given her two years before. One month before Alice's death, he wrote to Ollie, "Sweetheart, please do not speak of Christmas; it causes my heart to ache," and concluded, "Always yours, or no one's, Ollie." He wrote a love letter to Ollie the morning of the day of his wedding to Alice.[6] The two sides of his life, once so carefully bulkheaded, were converging and near collapse. Lemuel Johnson began to plan how to reduce his troubles by half.

Saturday night, December 15, 1917, was cold and cheerless in Richmond, with a high of only twenty-six degrees. "The sudden drop in the mercury last night served to keep the streets covered with a sheet of ice and made walking difficult," observed the *Times-Dispatch*.[7] Nevertheless, Alice Knight Johnson managed to slowly make her way the twelve blocks from her house at 1513 North Twenty-Second Street to the home of her friend Mrs. B.F. Stutz at 522 North Twenty-Seventh Street on Church Hill. Alice had last seen her new husband, Lemuel, on December 9, when he put her in a cab to take her home and boarded the midnight train to his parents' home in Middlesex, North Carolina.[8] Stuck in her parents' house due to the abysmal weather, Alice may have suffered from cabin fever, so the long walk through the icy streets of Church Hill was worth the chill.

Mrs. Stutz was an old friend from Alice's job at the Medical College, and the new bride apparently looked to Stutz as a mentor and confidante. In one of these conversations, Alice mentioned that she was on a regimen

522 North Twenty-Second Street, where Alice Johnson visited her friend Mrs. B.F. Stutz on December 15, 1917. Alice never left alive. *Author's photo.*

of medicine that her husband was giving her. Mrs. Stutz cautioned her about ruining her health by taking any medicine unnecessarily, but Alice replied that she was certainly not afraid "because the young doctor had mixed it himself."[9]

Also visiting Mrs. Stutz that evening was another friend, Mildred Taylor. The three ladies enjoyed a late supper, after which they chatted in front of the fireplace and Alice showed off some of the medicine prepared by her husband. She held out her pillbox for her friends' inspection, and one pill in the box was noticeably larger in comparison to the rest. "How can you swallow such a large one?" asked Taylor, and Alice laughingly replied, "Oh! This will knock 'L' out of me," and swallowed the pill. Her friends later recalled that within an hour, she excused herself and went to the bathroom for water. When she emerged, Alice gasped to her friends, "Oh, I am so sick." The girl collapsed, and when her friends rushed over to her, they could hear the growing hysteria in Alice's voice as she kept crying that she was experiencing a smothering sensation. The two horrified women watched helplessly as Alice gasped for breath and died within minutes.[10]

The lack of explanation as to what had caused her death hung over Alice's funeral on December 17. It was conducted in the parlor of Alice's parents' home on Twenty-Second Street, and the black-clad mourners spilled out into the cold and followed the coffin to the Knight family plot at Oakwood Cemetery. Among them was the grieving husband, Lemuel Johnson, who publicly called on the Richmond police to determine how Alice was given a poison pill with her usual medications. Two days after Alice's funeral, Lemuel again took a train to return to North Carolina to attend his ailing mother. Back in Richmond, Alice's grieving parents faced their first Christmas without their young daughter.[11]

Two days after the holiday, Detective Sergeants Wily and Smith, who were in charge of the investigation of Alice Johnson's death, had a conference with her parents at their home. Up to this point, her father and mother flatly refused to believe that Lemuel could be responsible for their daughter's death. But in the face of the evidence collected by the police, they began to come to an awful realization. "The father of Mrs. Johnson was the first of the family to lose faith in the young dentist, and last night as every circumstance in the case was unfolded, even the mother of the dead girl, who hitherto has maintained an unbounded confidence in the husband of her daughter, turned against him." Their only consolation may have been that disinterring Alice's body was not necessary to the case, mercifully sparing her parents that spectacle appearing in the press.[12]

At a rapid pace, Lemuel Johnson's life became publicly unglued and his secrets revealed after he left Richmond for North Carolina. Dr. A.F. Williams was summoned to Lemuel's room at the Briggs Hotel in Wilson and, upon entering, noticed the distinctive smell of prussic acid, a derivative of cyanide—the same poison found in Alice's stomach. Ironically, Lemuel was exhibiting the same symptoms that Alice's friends saw in her just before she collapsed and died.[13] He apparently did not take as large and potentially fatal a dose as Alice received in the pill that was prepared for her, and Dr. Williams immediately sent Lemuel to the local hospital for treatment.

Local police found the shaken and despondent Lemuel at the hospital and presented him with an arrest warrant for the murder of his wife, issued in Richmond. Asked by the police what this was all about, all the pale and nervous Lemuel could do was shake his head and mutter, "Troubles, troubles."[14]

Richmond authorities soon arrived in Wilson and took advantage of Lemuel's hospitalization to search the hotel room where he had been found. A packet of letters in his luggage revealed that not only had Lemuel been engaged to a Miss Ollie White since 1915, but in fact, this was also common knowledge in her North Carolina town. A shocked and humiliated Ollie White understandably pulled off the ring Lemuel had given her after the story of his betrayal reached her.[15] With the letters in Lemuel's hotel room where he had attempted suicide was a package with strict instructions that it be delivered only to the young dentist's mother. Inside was an engraved name plate surreptitiously pried from the lid of Alice's coffin and a ribbon that said simply "My Wife," from the flowers he sent to Alice's funeral.[16]

To the police and officials in Richmond, Lemuel's behavior after his arrest did not appear to be that of an innocent man, and Detective Wily later testified in court about his prisoner's behavior in the hospital. After he was confronted with the warrant from Richmond, Lemuel tried to jump out of the hospital window and repeatedly asked Wily for use of a straight razor. On the long train ride to Richmond and after sitting in silence for a while, Lemuel turned to Wily and asked, "What do you reckon they'll do to me, send me to the electric chair?" Wily, convinced that he was riding the train with a man who had murdered his young wife, only replied, "I can't tell anything about that."[17]

Lemuel Johnson arrived back in Richmond on Christmas Eve 1917 and was taken to police headquarters. Described as "pale and haggard," he was chain smoking and telling the police that he knew nothing about his wife's death or where the cyanide came from that killed her. Worn down from the tension of returning to Richmond and what he assumed would be his fate, Lemuel babbled to the police and newspapermen standing around the jail that insanity ran in his family and that his grandmother and brothers all suffered from "fits." "Alienists will doubtless be interested in the case on behalf of the accused man," predicted a newspaper account, using an early term for psychologists, "as his condition and acts invite the inspection of specialists."[18] Exhausted and still ill from the effects of ingesting poison, Lemuel was transported to the hospital area of the city jail.

The front page of the *Richmond Times-Dispatch* was filled with stories of hope and good cheer that Christmas morning. With the war in France on everyone's mind, thousands of patriotic Richmonders filled Broad Street at twilight and sang "America," followed by Christmas carols. A large photo in the newspaper showed Santa Claus visiting American soldiers in France, while an accounting of Richmond banks trumpeted healthy dividends and good prospects for 1918. Amid all the good cheer and upbeat news, an article on the front page about Lemuel Johnson and his suicide notes was a sobering contrast, with its words reflecting deep despair and betrayal.[19]

Once the accused dentist recovered from his self-poisoning, he was moved to a cell on the first floor of the jail. "According to his jailer, he is much improved in his condition and the rest seems to have given him a chance to get a grip on himself."[20]

Nevertheless, the release of these intimate snapshots of Lemuel's mental state must have been dismaying for the prisoner on both a personal and legal level, with his innermost thoughts exposed for the readers of newspapers in Richmond and beyond. The letters the police recovered in Lemuel's hotel room were clearly suicide notes to the people who mattered most in his confused mind. One letter was to his supposed fiancée Ollie White, one to his mother and one to Dr. S.V. Lewis, a friend. "Troubles and misfortune have overtaken me," wrote Lemuel to Ollie White, "and I can never bear to face them. You would never be happy should I live, so I am going to end my worried life, just to cause you to be happy in the future years.…Goodbye forever, Lemuel."[21]

To his mother, he wrote plaintively, "Dear Mamma: Here is the last letter from your loving son.…I wanted to be an honor to you, but a great trouble has overtaken me and I am not able to bear it." Lemuel confided to Dr. Lewis, "I have never loved but one, and want you to explain all things to her for my sake.…Try and protect my name."[22]

However, by the time Lemuel reached Richmond in the hands of the police, his story had changed completely, and the desperate tone of a man whose guilt was once such a burden that he attempted suicide was replaced by a flurry of explanations for his behavior. Sitting with an interviewer and chain-smoking cigarettes, he said that he had no recollection of writing letters to Ollie White, his North Carolina fiancée; his mother; or his friend Lewis. He said that he remembered White only as a friend and that the apparent suicide note addressed to her was only "the effect of excessive excitability as far as he is able to explain."[23]

In contrast, White announced that she would be traveling to Richmond to testify against Lemuel and declared to the press "the revelation of his duplicity drowned all affection for him," a phrase that hardly does justice to the wave of shame and embarrassment she must have felt. She added that Lemuel lied when he told her that a dear friend had dropped dead in a Richmond street, which covered the necessity of his abrupt departure to return for Alice's funeral. Ollie White, described as "attractive, if not real pretty, and is in no wise melancholy over the strange turn of affairs," was intent on revenge and grimly determined to see Lemuel brought to justice for his many lies to her.[24]

The year 1918 began as a busy season for sensational murders in central Virginia. In Goochland County, just west of Richmond, newspapers avidly followed the trial of Dr. Asa Chamberlain. The respected physician was accused of killing his brother, Albert, and burying his dismembered body in a pigpen behind his house. Richmond city coroner James Whitfield was an expert witness in that case, having the grim task of examining the body of a man whose spine and parts of his torso were buried in one location and whose "heart, arms, legs, heart, lungs, and parts of the intestines were found under fence posts" in the victim's brother's backyard.[25] In contrast, when Whitfield filled out the death certificate of Alice Johnson, he listed the cause of death as simply "apparent accidental poisoning by medicine."[26]

The lurid story of the murdered girl, apparently cruelly deceived by her malicious new husband, who was engaged to marry another and had just attempted to kill himself in a fit of guilt, had all the ingredients of a sensational thriller. Lemuel's suicide attempt and the betrayed fiancée living in North Carolina only added other salacious layers.

The tale of the pitiful Alice and her faithless husband captured the imagination of the press, and the story traveled across the country, spreading through the wire services. One newspaper said that the affair was attracting as much attention as the story of Thomas Cluverius, who famously murdered his pregnant cousin in 1885, or the shotgun murder of Louise Beattie outside Richmond on Midlothian Turnpike by her husband in 1911.[27] As with the account of Lemuel Johnson, those stories moved the usually staid city of Richmond into the uncomfortable glare of the national spotlight.

A flurry of delays and postponements meant that Lemuel Johnson's trial for Alice's murder did not begin until May 17, 1918. From the very start of the trial, Judge David Richardson had to take steps to maintain order in the crowded courtroom. "The crowd began to increase yesterday, and it was necessary for the court to instruct Sergeant Satterfield to direct spectators who had mounted window-sills in the hall outside the courtroom to get down."[28] At the same time, Richardson had to contend with complaints from the jurors, who were sequestered and complained bitterly of the meager two dollars per day allowed for meals and other necessities.[29]

Beside the practical necessities of his court, Judge Richardson made critical legal decisions that affected the course of the trial, such as the admissibility of the correspondence between Lemuel and Ollie White that formed the foundation of the Commonwealth's case against the young dentist. The letters were in a small canvas suitcase that had been removed from Lemuel's hotel room following his suicide attempt and subsequent arrest. Aside from the correspondence, in the bag was also a collection of totems that pointed to Lemuel's culpability: the plate from Alice's coffin, the ribbon from the flower arrangement he sent to her funeral and an embroidered handkerchief with Ollie White's name. Also in the little case was a watch fob purchased by Alice as a gift to Lemuel for the Christmas she did not live to see. When an attorney produced the pink ribbon from the suitcase, Lemuel was seen to dab at his eyes, and this little gesture on the part of the accused "is the only time he was observed emotionally reacting to the presentation of evidence."[30]

Some of the letters were deemed inadmissible by Judge Richardson, and these included those written by Ollie White to Lemuel, but the vast majority were allowed as evidence. "If the defense is able to break down the contention that the alleged engagement of Dr. Johnson to Miss Ollie White continued after his marriage to Alice Knight Johnson, the motive set up by the State will fall with it," observed one correspondent.[31]

The letters written from Lemuel to Ollie White certainly demonstrated Lemuel's devotion to her, before and during his marriage and after the sudden death of his wife. Members of the jury leaned forward with intense interest to hear the letters between Lemuel and Ollie White and the depths of his infatuation with her. The most famous of these letters was written on December 15 (the day of Alice's death), and it became known as the "Dearest Sweetheart" letter from its greeting. "Today is one that has taken all the joy taken out of my life"; Lemuel asked if she would blame him if he took something "to give him ease and a long sleep." The prosecution presented the correspondence between Lemuel and his love in North Carolina as the work of a young man playing a cynical game with the affections of two women. Lemuel's attempt to manage this intractable situation led to the only solution he could find after casually marrying Alice in Richmond. His despicable conduct was potently demonstrated by the prosecution, who read a letter to Ollie White written by Lemuel at 1:30 a.m. on September 18, 1917, gushing with his love for her. Incredibly, at 6:00 p.m. that same day, he married Alice Knight.[32]

Defense attorney Smith attempted to impart the letters with a lofty, romantic quality, comparing the "Dearest Sweetheart" letter to unsent lines written to an unrequited love. "People have written poetry to lady loves to whom they have never dared to express it," Smith said. Smith's honeyed attempt to characterize Lemuel's letters as lofty literature was jerked back into sharp contrast when Alice's mother was asked to identify the writing on the letter. Barbara Knight's voice rang out sharply in the courtroom. "It is Lemuel J. Johnson's," she said firmly.[33]

Mrs. Knight also provided some of the most damning testimony concerning what she was now sure was the death of her daughter at the hands of her new husband. Heavily veiled, Knight took the witness stand and described Lemuel's offhand way of asking for her daughter's hand by making her "a Tarheel," which Mrs. Knight thought was a flippant manner of addressing her on such an important occasion.

She also recalled the last time Alice saw Lemuel after he put her in a cab to take her home the evening he left for North Carolina. That night, Alice returned to Church Hill with "an intense burning sensation in her stomach" that was never explained.[34] Mrs. Knight also recounted how odd it seemed, standing beside Lemuel at Alice's coffin and turning sharply to look at him after she heard the prayer he made under his breath: "O God, forgive me and make me a better man."[35]

Mrs. Knight recalled going through her daughter's clothes, searching for a burial dress and in the process finding a handkerchief embroidered with the name "Ollie White." The handkerchief went missing after Lemuel spent a night in his wife's room at his in-laws' home, and it later became a key piece of evidence at trial. The handkerchief was also the focus of the testimony of Alice's eleven-year-old brother, Brandon, who slept in his sister's room with Lemuel the night after her death. Brandon Knight told the court that he had woken in the middle of the night and watched Lemuel silently search Alice's room for something (presumably the damning handkerchief), fruitlessly looking through all the dresser drawers and closets with a flashlight. The boy was said to respond with an easy calmness, even in the face of attorney John Woodward's "stern" cross-examination. In his child's voice, Brandon Knight painted a vivid picture of the furtive Lemuel, frantically searching his dead wife's room while he thought his juvenile brother-in-law was asleep.[36]

Various other witnesses testified specifically about the effects of Lemuel's prescriptions for his hapless bride. Mary Jordan was a friend of Alice's who lived at 1508 North Twenty-Second Street, just a few doors away from the Knight home. She testified that Alice told Jordan that Lemuel had given Alice some "strong medicine" that made her sick on Monday, December 10, and she was supposed to take another dose a few days later. J.R. McCauley, secretary of the Medical College of Virginia, said that Alice was still ill on December 11 while she was at work. McCauley added a poignant note that the doomed Alice was "generally bright and cheerful and was not at all downcast on the afternoon of the Saturday on which she died."[37]

Coroner Whitfield took the stand and said that he had found a quantity of prussic acid, a cyanide derivative, in Alice's stomach during his extensive investigation of her death. On a macabre note, Whitfield, who was also a professor at the Medical College of Virginia, described exhibiting the stomach for his chemistry class and mentioned offhandedly that both Dr. Johnson and Miss Knight, as she was called at the school, were both well known by the same students now regarding her dissected stomach.[38]

The last witness for the state was Mrs. Stutz, Alice's friend, who described the second occasion when she met Lemuel and their odd conversation. The otherwise innocuous chat turned to the subject of predestination, and Mrs. Stutz remarked that she believed everyone was predestined to die in a certain way. Seizing on the idea, Lemuel asked, "Why should a murderer be held responsible, if the Lord intended them to die by the hands of a murderer?" Mrs. Stutz's stunned response wasn't recorded, but in retrospect, the question was chillingly ironic.[39]

"A throng larger than on any day since the case began last Wednesday crowded into the small Hustings Court chamber yesterday. Spectators lined the walls, crammed the doorways, and a number sat on the steps of the bench occupied by Judge Richardson and lined the wall behind the upraised landing on which the judge was seated."[40] The only person barred from the proceedings was A. Cloyd Gill, a special correspondent of the *Washington Times*, sent to Richmond to cover the sensational trial of Lemuel Johnson. Gill claimed to have visited Lemuel in the Richmond jail and obtained a complete confession from him. However, the accused murderer never signed it and later noted that while Gill had interviewed him, he had not confessed to Alice's poisoning.[41] Gill was later put on the stand, and it was revealed that he was not in Richmond during the time the alleged confession took place. Because of the allegations and controversy swirling around Gill and the unsigned confession, Judge Richardson did not allow the confession to be used as evidence, and the ambitious newspaperman had to wait outside except when it was his turn to testify.[42]

After several motions for delay of the trial, on the morning of May 25, 1918, Judge Richardson convened his court and warned the packed room that he demanded total silence from the crowd. Lemuel Johnson took the stand from 11:30 a.m. that morning until court adjourned six hours later. Speaking calmly and with a slight speech impediment, the defendant told the story of his life up to the point where he had been arrested, only showing emotion or tears when speaking of Alice. He dismissed his relationship with Ollie White as one that had persisted since they had been childhood friends. He related the perfect storm of "over-study in his dental course, his mother critically ill, about to be inducted into the National Army and nervousness as the result of the loss of sleep" that led him to take poison in his hotel room. He admitted that he wrote the letters discussing his impending suicide attempt but had no memory of doing that or taking poison. "I had worried until I was absent-minded," Lemuel told the jury, as the explanation for his behavior. Lemuel denied the incident sworn to by Alice's mother where he prayed for forgiveness beside his wife's open coffin and denied ever owning cyanide.[43]

The following day, Lemuel was questioned for five hours straight by Commonwealth's Attorney Wise but stuck to his story and explained away all the damning circumstances presented by other witnesses. "He stuck almost unfalteringly to the tale he had been told by his council, John E. Woodard of Wilson, N.C., and made a favorable impression on the throng which packed the courtroom almost to suffocation."[44] Lemuel explained away his search for the handkerchief, saying that Alice's little brother saw him just looking for a coat hanger. The awkward packet of items like the plate from Alice's coffin and the ribbon that said "My Wife" that he had in his possession was a simple mistake in packing.

Lemuel said that A. Cloyd Gill, the Washington reporter, had advised him to plead guilty and offered him $100 to sign a confession. As to the suddenness of his marriage to Alice, Lemuel claimed that he did not realize he was going to be married that same day when he had written to Ollie White. Mrs. Knight, suspicious that he had poisoned Alice on more than one occasion, asked Lemuel directly, "What did you give Alice?" and Lemuel repeated his response, "Nothing." Every damning circumstance regarding the timing of his marriage, his relationship with Ollie White, the purchase of cyanide and Lemuel's suicide attempt were all skillfully defused under the direction of Lemuel's lawyer. No explanation was offered for passages in the letters written by Lemuel to Ollie White with such loaded phrases as "Tonight Lemuel is a better boy than ever before" and "my whole life has been changed."

Lemuel's lawyer even managed to deflect the significance of a letter written by Lemuel to E.C. White, Ollie White's father, who apparently despised the young man and threatened to shoot Lemuel if he came to the White home again. "I will not stop going with her under any circumstances," wrote Lemuel, twelve days before Alice's death. Lemuel's defiance was based, he said, on an insulting remark that Mr. White had made about the young man, who had taken offense and was trying to appear defiant.[45]

Commonwealth's Attorney Wise delivered what was termed "a scathing arraignment of the dentist" that lasted two hours as his closing argument, but it was futile. After fourteen days of testimony, the jury only deliberated for an hour and ten minutes. In the case of *The Commonwealth v. Lemuel Johnson*, they declared him innocent and a free man. Judge David Richardson again cautioned the court that he wanted no reaction when the verdict was read, but the estimated one hundred people in the room burst into cheers. "There must have been two hundred people who came up and shook my hand and congratulated me," said Lemuel, who left court and went to the home at 120 North Lombardy Street, where he had boarded as a dental student.

"'That looks good to me' smilingly commented Dr. Lemuel J. Johnson as his fingers traced the word 'acquitted' in the State Special edition of the *Times-Dispatch* last night."[46] Commenting on the arguments that might have sent him to the electric chair, Lemuel was quoted, "'Mr. Wise says I am an educated man; Mr. Smith says I am no fool; Dr. Freeman says there is something the matter with me, but he isn't smart enough to know what it is,' and with this, the young dentist laughed heartily."[47]

Despite his happy reaction to being acquitted of murder, the strain of the trial apparently took a toll on Lemuel Johnson. A North Carolina newspaper reported that he was still in Richmond on June 1 and on the verge of "a nervous collapse."[48]

Lemuel returned to North Carolina but did not marry the professed love of his life, Ollie White. In 1922, she married Roscoe Pierce and moved to Franklin County, North Carolina, where she was a music teacher until her death in 1969.[49]

Lemuel established a dental practice in his hometown of Middlesex and married a woman named Lena Snells in 1924. However, happiness did not follow for the young man despite the success of his business.[50] Perhaps he did feel, as he mentioned to Mrs. Stutz, that his was the hand of inevitable fate and that Alice was bound for Oakwood Cemetery at a young age no matter what course her life took. Or perhaps he was forever haunted by the face of his nineteen-year-old bride smiling up at him with trust and confidence and Alice good-naturedly beaming at the thought of the possibilities of their new married life.

The week before Thanksgiving 1925 was cool and clear in Nash County, North Carolina. On November 18, Lemuel Johnson came out on the front porch of his parents' house and briefly surveyed the yard and the sky. He then produced a revolver from his pocket, pressed the muzzle against his head, closed his eyes and pulled the trigger.

Back in Richmond, a newspaper article about the suicide of the once-notorious North Carolina dentist recounted Alice's death and her husband's trial for her murder. The article hinted darkly at Lemuel's past and implied that his guilt finally caught up with him: "No reason is known for the deed,

Right: This weathered slab of concrete covers the grave of Lemuel Johnson in Nash County, North Carolina. *William Kemp.*

Below: The grave of Alice Knight Johnson at Richmond's Oakwood Cemetery. *Author's photo.*

but Dr. Johnson had seemed depressed for some time, and it is believed that some secret trouble was preying on his mind."[51] The Nash County coroner who filled out his death certificate bluntly stated Lemuel's cause of death as "shot self in head." The coroner also calculated that the dentist lived thirty-two years, eight months and eleven days.[52]

Today, it isn't easy to find the last resting place of Alice Knight and her parents. Their headstones are slowly sinking in the grass of Richmond's Oakwood Cemetery, and at first glance, the Knight plot appears empty. Barbara Knight died at age forty-eight in early 1925, too soon to hear of the suicide of her former son-in-law, but George Knight lived until 1929 and may have taken some grim satisfaction from reading the reports from North Carolina about Lemuel's death. The Knight family—mother, father and young daughter—have been there under their blanket of green for one hundred years. Still, the determined visitor can brush the grass away to reveal the marker the grieving parents chose for their once-cheerful child, the sad victim of a heartless young man who once swore to protect and love her:

> *Our Alice*
> *Age 19 Yrs.*
> *Blessed are the pure*
> *of heart for they*
> *shall see God.*

Chapter 2

A JUMP OR A FALL?

THE HORRIFIC SUICIDE OF JAMES MONROE WINSTEAD

When *A History of the Government of the City of Richmond* was published in 1899, the building now known as Old City Hall had been completed only five years before. The new city hall was the proud statement that this was a triumphant, modern city that built a railroad hub and manufacturing center on the foundation of its war-torn and storied past. Oddly, the otherwise relentlessly upbeat *History of the Government of the City of Richmond* noted two dark days in the life of the young city hall, both involving suicides.[53]

Alfred P. Shield was a former city official who had been dismissed from his post in the Revenue Department, which collected city taxes. He was once an actor who toured with the famous Edwin Booth but later returned to Richmond and was employed by the city.[54] In January 1896, he entered a hardware store on Broad Street and purchased a small amount of .38-caliber ammunition. Walking down to city hall, Shield entered the building, walked up the wide stairs to the second floor and locked himself in a room. Firing a bullet into the woodwork and apparently being satisfied that the revolver worked, Shield stuck it in his mouth and pulled the trigger.[55] "Mr. Alfred P. Shield, who shot himself in the City Hall building on Thursday, was able to sit up awhile yesterday.…The injured man is taking nourishment regularly, and is believed to be steadily improving," was reported on January 12.[56] Instead, Shield lingered until dying on January 28, leaving behind a devastated widow and four children. His unmarked grave is in his grandfather's plot at Shockoe Hill Cemetery.

As shocking as the Shield suicide was, it was done privately, and the victim died surrounded by family in the quiet of a hospital room. Nothing could possibly be different than the circumstances of the very public and sensational suicide of James Monroe Winstead two years earlier. Far from a lingering death, Winstead died in seconds on August 23, 1894, in front of horrified witnesses who just happened to have the bad luck of being at Tenth and Broad Streets that morning.

Ford's Hotel stood north of Capitol Square and south of Broad Street, in the block just east of the city hall. Ford's was popular with generations of traveling businessmen and was a famous home away from home for Virginia politicians from across the state when the legislature was in session. It was a natural choice for James Winstead, a successful businessman, entrepreneur and bank president who was visiting Richmond from his home in Greensboro, North Carolina. Winstead's wife and three stepchildren did not accompany him on his trip to Richmond, but instead stayed in Greensboro.[57] In light of what happened the morning after Winstead's arrival in Richmond, his demeanor was later closely examined for clues of his inexplicable behavior. The astonishing contrast between the arrival of the perfectly calm and polite visitor from Greensboro one day and how he left Richmond the next was as perplexing as it was shocking in the grim determination beneath that gentility.

Winstead retired to his room after arriving in Richmond on the afternoon of September 12, 1894, and registering at Ford's Hotel, receiving the key to room 167. "He rose quite early yesterday morning and was about the office of the hotel before the breakfast hour, and spoke pleasantly to several persons," reported the *Richmond Dispatch*. "His demeanor at the breakfast table was natural, and he ate a good breakfast."[58] Winstead ran into an acquaintance from Greensboro in the lobby and chatted with him. "His conversation was that of a well-balanced, courteous business man, and Mr. Garret saw nothing in his manner to indicate that the banker premeditated the tragic end to his life that followed less than an hour afterward."[59]

Winstead walked across Eleventh Street to the city hall, entered the east door, crossed the ornate lobby and rode the elevator to the topmost floor. The city hall clock tower was home to the Fire Alarm Office, where dozens of wires led to the alarm apparatus and the tower itself served as a fire lookout. The area above that level, where the actual clock mechanism drove the hands of the four huge clock faces, was intended as an observation deck and was popular with visitors to Richmond who braved its height to look down on the city.[60] Winstead asked the janitor for the key to the observation

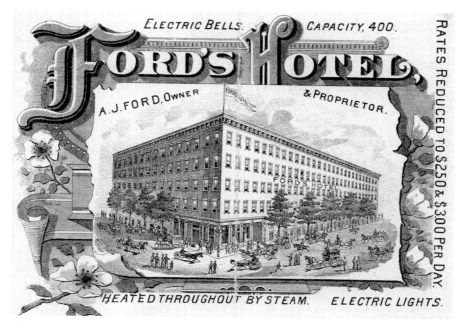

Ford's Hotel, where Winstead spent his last night. *Author's collection.*

deck and climbed the spiral cast-iron stairs to that topmost level of the tower.[61] "The keys were procured for him and he was given some instruction as to closing the windows and doors when he left the tower. He showed no signs whatever of being excited and proceeded to the tower above."[62]

Winstead, overweight and seventy years old, was forced to use a nearby stepladder to cross over a low partition, emerging on a narrow granite balcony whose railing was just below waist height. Below him, Broad Street was teeming with pedestrians, horse-drawn carriages and wagons as far as the eye could see. The clatter and sounds of Broad Street may have been muted to Winstead, ninety-five feet above the street, who slipped out of his shoes and threw them, his hat and his cane over the balcony. Seconds later, he jumped off.

W.H. Hannaford was standing at the corner of Tenth and Broad Streets, across from the city hall clock tower. He happened to glance up at the clock and noticed "an old gentleman in the granite balcony of the tower on the Broad street side. While I was looking I saw him plunge headlong over the stone balustrade. He fell with terrific speed...and the next moment was quivering on the sharp points of the iron rails which guard the area immediately under the private office of the City Treasurer."[63] Standing

Above: Richmond's ornate 1894 city hall. Winstead jumped from one of the clock tower's small balconies, ninety-five feet above the sidewalk. *Author's photo*.

Opposite: The view from the balcony where Winsted jumped. The cast-iron fence he landed on is directly below. *Author's photo*.

across Broad Street, eleven-year-old Wille Dunsford made the mistake of looking up at the clock at the same time and said he saw Winstead drop his shoes, hat and cane off the balcony and immediately jump headfirst.[64] Henry Brown worked as a street sprinkler for the city, keeping the dust down in the late summer Richmond heat. He was drawing water at the corner of Broad and Twelfth and glanced up at the clock to check the time. He saw "the old gentleman" on the balcony and watched as he jumped off. "He went tolerably straight until he reached the lower balcony; his body struck and whirled rapidly until arrested by the railing."[65]

Richmond city treasurer Charles H. Phillips was in his office and out of the corner of his eye saw something crossing his window at terrific speed before hearing the impact of Winstead's body. Rushing outside, he found a crowd gathered around the body, impaled on the fence. "The head and body hung downward inside the iron fence and over the mouth of the area. It was suspended from one of the sharp spears, which had caught the left leg just at the hip joint, as the body fell face downward, and the force of the fall had torn it entirely out of the socket. This hung over the side of the railing next [to] the sidewalk."[66]

City Coroner Dr. William H. Taylor arrived, took one look at the body of Winstead, "crushed into almost to a shapeless mass," and decided that neither a postmortem nor inquest would be necessary. He had the mutilated body moved to the undertaking establishment of Langdon Christian, a few blocks east at 1215 East Broad Street.[67]

For many, the notion that Winstead killed himself was beyond comprehension. "Greensboro people are inclined to believe the fall accidental and not a suicide," reported a North Carolina newspaper, adding, "Col. Winstead's business is thought to be in good shape. His domestic relations were very pleasant."[68] In Winston-Salem, the *Western Sentinel* said that people in his hometown were indignant at the idea that such a prominent citizen would travel to Richmond to commit suicide, and Greensboro rose to the defense of the corpulent Winstead: "It has been his custom, they say, for several years to remove his shoes, coat and hat whenever he became very warm. He was so fleshy and particularly affected that he became over-heated more easily than most people. On this occasion he had just climbed up the tower—a tiresome undertaking for a man of his size—and according to his custom, removed coat, shoes, and hat to catch the morning breezes....The cause of Col. Winstead's fall, they think, was purely accidental, occasioned by his leaning forward to inspect some part of the building below or a distant object. Vertigo may have seized him in the act."[69]

The horrific nature of Winstead's death, contrasted with the inexplicable circumstances and otherwise mundane path that led him to Richmond's city hall, became a news item across the country as various newspapers picked up the story. The *Atlanta Constitution* carried the news as a deliberate death but noted that Winstead was being stoutly defended by friends and family as being a victim of vertigo.[70] In Baltimore, Winstead's death was flatly termed a suicide by the evidence of his hat and cane. "They struck the sidewalk about two seconds before the body. This fact precludes the idea that the fall was an accident," but it was admitted the suicide was "a mystery."[71] The *San Francisco Chronicle* featured the story of Winstead's death the very next day. The paper described Winstead's nephew, E.D. Winstead, who had returned to Greensboro with the body, as not accepting the explanation of suicide, saying that his uncle was in "comfortable circumstances financially and had no domestic troubles." Winstead's taking his shoes off on the balcony was due, the nephew said, to the fact that he suffered from "rheumatism in his feet." The reporter following the story in far-off California may have been the most succinct when he remarked of Winstead that "his preparations were apparently made with the coolest deliberation and his procedure to end his existence marked with the most solid determination."[72]

Winstead's hat, shoes and cane arriving on the Broad Street sidewalk just before his body hit the fence remained the most telling evidence that the banker had killed himself. Charles Phillips noticed Winstead's hat falling past his first-floor window first, followed within seconds by its owner. Despite his loyal North Carolina friends defending Winstead as the victim of an accident, "it cannot be understood why he dropped his shoes, hat and cane before he himself fell. If the articles spoken of had started from the balcony simultaneously the latter would certainly have reached the ground first," reasoned a Richmond reporter.[73]

John Mitchell Jr. was a leader of Richmond's African American community, publisher and president of Jackson Ward's Mechanics Savings Bank. Mitchell was no friend of the white banking establishment arrayed along Main Street and apparently had little sympathy for suicides. Writing on the editorial page of his newspaper, the *Richmond Planet*, Mitchell noted that "a white bank president jumped from the City Hall tower on the iron spikes of the railings below. We said he was white; no colored man would be as big a fool as that."[74]

Statistics compiled in Richmond seemed to confirm Mitchell's wry statement. Six weeks before Winstead's fall, the *Richmond Dispatch* printed an article on its front page cheerfully titled "Hints to Suicides" and subtitled "The Most Popular Methods Employed by People Taking Their Lives." The piece was an odd combination of tongue-in-cheek observations about popular ways to kill one's self combined with statistics of how Richmonders usually accomplished that goal. "What I have to say on the subject of suicide," wrote the unknown author, who signed the story "E.G.R.," "is mainly the result of a conversation I had with that ever bright and witty scholar, Coroner William H. Taylor."[75] Dr. Taylor may have later regretted being so witty on the subject of suicide as he regarded the mess that had been James Monroe Winstead displayed on the tines of a city hall fence.

After a discussion of various methods ("Death by poison, drowning, or suffocation is far more preferable than any other"), the author of the article in the *Richmond Dispatch* presents figures that seem to validate John Mitchell Jr.'s editorial opinion. The *Dispatch* printed a "tabulated score of suicidal performances" of self-destruction in Richmond for the previous twenty-two years. It being Richmond, the information was segregated by race, showing a total of eighty-six people having committed suicide: seventy-six white people and ten "colored." The article continues with more gallows humor on the subject of suicide, but readers of the *Dispatch* must have recalled the article that ran the month before as a distasteful portent of the dreadful display at city hall a few weeks later.[76]

The tines of the cast-iron fence where Winstead fell are still bent from the impact, testifying to his dramatic death. *Author's photo.*

Back in Greensboro, the city's newspapers loyally came to the defense of Winstead. "There seems to be no ground for the theory he took his own life. No motive for such a rash act can be discovered. His finances were in such a condition to cause him little or no concern, while his family relations were of the pleasantest and most harmonious character," stoutly maintained the *Greensboro Patriot*.[77] Winstead famously sold his interest in a wholesale drug firm that eventually became Coca-Cola for $10,000 two years before his death.[78]

Of more importance to the city of Greensboro was that Winstead was president of both the State Bank and the Piedmont Bank of that city, and both institutions were immediately thrown into suspicion. North Carolinians, like the rest of the country, well recalled the economic depression that became known as the Panic of 1873 that started with a chain of bank failures and whose effects lingered for years afterward. In the days before deposit insurance, customers had to know that the leadership of their bank was just as personally stable as the granite, brass and steel architecture that enclosed their money. The suicide of the bank president could easily be interpreted as signaling imminent bank failure and complete disaster for the depositors. Both Greensboro banks immediately let it be known that their books were in good order, there was no malfeasance and the institutions were as sound as their president apparently had been when he boarded the train for Richmond.[79]

Winstead's battered remains were accompanied back to Greensboro by his loyal nephew the day after his death, and his funeral was held that afternoon. An account from Greensboro was printed in the Raleigh newspaper, still in the telegraphic style in which it was received: "The remains of Col. Winstead arrived this morning. The funeral took place at 4 o'clock this afternoon and was largely attended." The reporter concluded the brief article by repeating the theory that Winstead was a victim of vertigo.[80]

James Monroe Winstead took the explanation for his grisly end with him to his grave under a shady canopy of trees at Greensboro's Green Hill Cemetery. It is a little-known facet of Richmond's long and storied history that there is still a record in cast iron of the split second when Winstead landed on the fence. The accounts from the time carefully specify which fence Winstead landed on, and the tines there are still bent from the impact, almost 130 years later.

Standing on the Broad Street sidewalk, you can look straight up at the granite tower above you and almost hear the clatter of a man's cane hit the sidewalk. Immediately afterward, above, the widening silhouette of a body hurtling down, twisting in the air, blocking out the Richmond sky. The reason for Colonel Winstead's dramatic end—be it vertigo, self-destruction, leaning too far over the low balcony or a chance gust of wind—will never be known. The intervening 116 years since Winstead made his way up to the city hall clock tower has made this once sensational and very public death the tiniest of footnotes in Richmond's long history. Nevertheless, the bent tines of the cast-iron railing where Winstead's body was impaled remain today as mute witness to a morning's violence on Broad Street and the inexplicable and dramatic end of a visitor from North Carolina.

Chapter 3

MURDERED IN MIDSTREAM

THE TWO LOVES OF AMOS HADLEY

The intersection of Westham Station Road and Old Bridge Lane is not one of Henrico County's more notable suburban crossroads. The only distinctive feature is a nearby one-lane bridge over the Kanawha Canal; the once-busy canal today serves only to bring water to the city. In the distance, a disused road leads to the site of the Westham Bridge, demolished fifty years ago. Beyond that, there is a double set of train tracks, and the small train station that once stood at this crossing is also long gone. There is not a lot to see at this intersection, but once, one hundred years ago, a man stood at this place with his wife and made a decision that would end both their lives. Had the couple taken the road to the right at this crossroads on that winter day, it would have led up the hill toward lights, warmth and safety. Instead, he directed her to the left—across the canal and onto the literal road to darkness, madness and murder.

The commencement exercises at Richmond College (now the University of Richmond) in May 1918 were bittersweet for the graduates as the school prepared to leave the campus. As part of the war effort that supported the troops fighting in France, the school vacated its facility in Henrico County and turned it over to the War Department as a hospital. Many of the students would soon be drafted to serve in the army, destined to be scattered across the country for training, while the remainder moved into classrooms set up in makeshift locations in the city, like the old St. Luke's Hospital on West Grace Street.

Dr. Amos Hadley (1882–1921), a talented surgeon and anesthesiologist, sociopath and murderer. *Author's collection.*

By the following July, the transformation of the Richmond College buildings was complete, and the new Westhampton Hospital established on the former college campus was ready to receive its first two hundred patients.[81] Trains of wounded arrived on the same spur track that entered the campus at the intersection of Huguenot Road and River Road that is now called the University of Richmond "Eco-Corridor." Today, those strolling the neatly landscaped path that was the old rail bed would be surprised to find that this was once where drab green rail cars unloaded a grim cargo of wounded, blinded and maimed young men. The trains of wounded kept arriving, and Westhampton Hospital eventually housed one thousand patients in the former dormitories and classrooms.[82]

Among the staff caring for patients at Westhampton Hospital was Dr. Wilmer Amos Hadley, age thirty-nine, a native of central Kansas who had been raised in a Quaker colony in Friendswood, Texas. Dr. Hadley practiced medicine in Colorado and was educated for military medical service at a school in Chattanooga, where he placed sixth in a class of one thousand students. After he was commissioned a lieutenant, he was assigned to an army facility in Charlotte, North Carolina, before transferring to the new hospital in Richmond and moving to the city with his wife.[83]

Sue Kathleen Tinsley, the daughter of a prominent architect in Cincinnati, Ohio, was born in 1870. She became an accomplished musician and a teacher of voice and instruments. While touring Texas, she met Amos Hadley, and they were married in 1913 and moved to Colorado. However, in July 1918, Dr. Hadley met and fell deeply in love with a young nurse, Gladys Mercer, at the new hospital in Richmond. At first, he did not tell her that he was married and lived with his wife five miles from the hospital. Hadley finally confessed to his girlfriend, but he assured Mercer that his wife was going to California to secure a divorce. Hadley told Mercer about putting his wife on the train headed west, and on the strength of his assurances, he and Gladys became engaged. Hadley left Richmond on December 6 and later that week wrote to Mercer from Atlanta and then Texas with the details of his wife's sudden death in California.[84] Gladys Mercer would not see her would-be fiancé again for more than two years.

Westhampton Hospital, having served its purpose, was closed in March 1919; the facilities were dismantled, and the equipment was shipped to other hospitals. Fifty-six staff members received their discharges and returned to their homes. Among them was Gladys Mercer, who moved back to Brooklyn.[85] She and Amos Hadley continued to correspond, his letters often beginning, "Dear Honey-bird." Before Gladys left Richmond, Hadley gave her an engagement ring, and they made plans to be married on April 20, 1919. His letters to her, often using the pledge "You are the only girl in the world for me," were filled with plans to quit his practice and described the life they would have together on his ranch in Texas. At the end of 1918, he gave her a watch that was engraved, "Gladys, may all the coming years be bright as this Christmas Day."[86] The couple's future looked rosy for the new year of 1919.

Susan Tinsley Hadley (1870–1918). Devoted to her husband, she became the victim of a heartless murder in his hands. *Author's collection.*

To ensure that the women in Hadley's dual life never encountered each other, he told his wife that hospital regulations forbade her from visiting him at work or even telephoning. Sadly, the time he spent cheating on his wife was interpreted by her as dedication to his practice, and Sue Hadley always said how proud she was of the long hours he worked, to the point of being home only a few days a week.[87] Sue "appeared to be intensely in love with her husband, often dwelling upon his arduous duties which kept them apart so much."[88] Because of her blind devotion, an outing on a winter afternoon with her husband must have been very appealing for Sue Hadley.

Their next-door neighbor, Mrs. Arthur King, recalled the last time she saw Mrs. Hadley, on November 2, 1918. She was in a hurry, King recollected, saying that she was going for a car ride with her husband—a rare treat. Eugene Fergusson ran a Richmond cab service and recalled being hired by Hadley to take the doctor and his wife out to a home on the south side of the river, near Bon Air. The car wound out Cary Street Road and down the hill beside the Country Club of Virginia but got stuck in the lowlands near Westham Creek (where the River Road Shopping Center now stands). The couple got out of the car and walked toward the Westham Bridge along what is now known as Westham Station Road.[89]

Rollin Eppes was cutting wood in the river bottom that day and had a wagon loaded and ready to take back to Richmond. A passing coal train stopped him at the Westham Station crossing, and while he waited, he noticed the gentleman in an army officer's uniform and a "white lady" talking as they stood on the other side of the tracks. As the train roared through the crossing, Eppes noticed the lady silently put her arm through the officer's arm and drew him to her. After the train passed and the pair approached him, he heard the man say, "I'll get this boy to help me." Eppes followed the couple to the riverbank and helped Hadley lug a canoe out of a shed near the bridge abutment and launch it; then he helped the lady get seated in it. Eppes later testified that this was the last he saw of them, the boat drifting quietly away from the bank through the floating leaves.[90]

Later that afternoon, Dr. Hadley returned to his home on West Grace Street. He told his landlady, Mrs. Evans, that they had met friends from Pittsburgh who were on a motor tour of Virginia who had persuaded Sue to join them. At the time, Mrs. Evans thought it odd that the fastidious Mrs. Hadley did not appear to have taken any clothing or belongings with her

Rollin Eppes saw Dr. and Mrs. Hadley standing at the end of this bridge, waiting for a train to pass, and noticed her hook her arm in his. *Author's photo.*

on this trip. Three days later, Amos Hadley returned and reported to the landlady that Sue was having a "bully time" on her trip to Pennsylvania, and he wasn't sure when she would return. He said Sue mentioned in a letter that she was writing to Mrs. Evans, but that letter never arrived.[91]

As he packed his suitcase, Dr. Hadley told Evans that he was waiting for his formal discharge from Westhampton Hospital. What she remembered most vividly was that as they chatted, Amos Hadley "threw every toilet article, including perfumes, powders, toilet waters and other intimate boudoir effects belonging to Mrs. Hadley into a waste basket." Confused, Evans later rescued the items from the trash and kept them for Sue Hadley to reclaim those dressing table items, which would later be turned over to the police used as evidence. Hadley secured his discharge from Westhampton Hospital on December 5, 1918. He returned to the Clark house with an army truck, loaded up a trunk and the rest of his belongings and drove away. Mrs. Evans never saw Dr. Hadley again.[92]

Hadley visited W.W. Foster's studio November 29, 1918, and had his photograph taken, perhaps as what he knew would be a going-away gift to his fiancée.[93] In the photograph, Hadley's expression conveys very little, with an air of professional neutrality that he may have learned at many hospital bedsides. Or perhaps it is the studied, emotionless and focused look of a sociopathic murderer. Hadley was photographed in his military physician's uniform, adorned with only the "U.S." pin and the medical caduceus symbol on each collar. The collar itself looks disheveled, and the famously tidy Dr. Hadley had it carelessly fastened above the top button of his tunic. A small band of white indicates an undergarment is sticking out of the right side of his collar. In light of Hadley's rapid departure from Richmond a few days later, the state of his dress, especially for a formal portrait, signals haste and an indication that the once-impeccable subject had become indifferent to his appearance in uniform. Behind his pince-nez, Hadley's light-colored eyes betray nothing about the man who cruelly murdered his wife just weeks before this image was made.

The momentous year of 1918 was drawing to a close when Peter Miles entered the woods west of the Westham Bridge to check on his traps. December 31 was a cold morning, and Miles noticed an overcoat waving in the clear current. Peering into the water, he realized that there was something substantial filling the coat: a dead woman lodged under the surface, her limbs twisted in an awkward pose. Recoiling, Miles ran through the woods to the Westham train station, where there was a telephone, and the Henrico County authorities were soon alerted.[94]

Detective Captain Alex Wright of the Richmond police also came to the site, where he met Henrico County sheriff Sydnor, several Henrico deputies and the county coroner, J. Fulmer Bright. The woman's body was frozen stiff and bore no identifying papers or jewelry, and the fingers of the glove on her hand had been ripped, as though rings may have been torn off in haste. She was wearing a man's overcoat, black gloves, a sweater and a dress, as well as a disturbing addition to her wardrobe: a length of heavy wire twisted around her waist. "Signs point to foul play," said Coroner Bright grimly, "and the case looks bad." The police looked for clues in the area around where the body was found and searched the riverbank for a half mile in either direction until nightfall. The frozen corpse was put into a wagon and taken to the Arthur Neilson Funeral Home in Fulton for examination.[95]

"Richmond Greets New Year Quietly" read the headline in a newspaper, as 1919 began on a somber note with rain dampening the usual outdoor celebrations in the city. The article described a morose and subdued city where, "[w]ith a heroic attempt at the cheer of departed days, Richmond this morning ushered into the halls of time a new babe, who smiles upon a world at peace and is christened Nineteen Nineteen." The winter gloom complemented the lurid, front-page report of the examination of the body from the river. The removal of the clothes from the corpse was difficult, as "they were covered with mud and leaves matted together and frozen. Several times a hammer had to be used to knock off ice which clung around parts of the body."[96] Newspaper coverage was merciless in detailing the victim's corpse: "There were no rings on her fingers. Her hair had matted and frozen and had fallen from the scalp." "The color of her eyes," specified the article, "was blue."[97]

Several people called at the coroner's office inquiring about daughters or sisters who were missing. A Richmond mother thought it was her errant daughter, and a telegram arrived from Georgia asking "for a description, particularly as to the color of the dead woman." A Mr. Hallbrook in Washington reported that his sister disappeared on December 13 and that the body could be hers. Richmond police investigated the case of a local department store clerk who had not been seen for several weeks but were unable to make any of these connections with the body from the river.[98]

It was Dr. Hadley's landlady, Mrs. Evans, who after comparing notes with other women in her neighborhood who knew Sue Hadley took on the dreadful task of viewing the corpse held at the morgue. This was not an easy job after the body had been in the James River for six weeks. Despite the sight of the distorted and bloated body of her former tenant, distinctive repairs

Mrs. Evans had made to some of the clothing the corpse wore confirmed that these were indeed the pitiful remains of Sue Hadley.[99]

After inquiries began as to the whereabouts of Dr. Hadley, a telegram was received by his brother-in-law, a prominent Cincinnati businessman named A.H. Evans. Hadley wrote to Evans from Atlanta on December 5, the day after Hadley's discharge from the army and just two days after disappearing from Richmond. Hadley said that he had bad news and that Sue became ill with influenza during a visit to Puerto Rico and died on November 24. She was buried, Hadley said, at the American Cemetery in San Juan. Evans dutifully took out the following obituary, which appeared on December 10 in the *Cincinnati Enquirer*: "HADLEY—Sue Tinsley Hadley, beloved wife of Dr. W.A. Hadley and sister of Mrs. A.H. Evans. November 23, 1918, at San Juan, Porto [*sic*] Rico."[100] Hadley wrote again from Texas, three days after Sue Hadley's body was found but before it was identified. This letter also expressed Hadley's anguish over the death of his wife.[101]

His sister-in-law, Mrs. A.H. Evans, mistrusted Amos Hadley and couldn't imagine that Sue would have gone to Puerto Rico without writing to her first. Sue's sister had a letter from her as recently as November 9, when Sue mentioned that her husband was leaving Westhampton Hospital and that she and Amos were going to New York for the holidays. The sisters planned to see each other after that, as Sue and Amos would visit Cincinnati on their way to his home in Texas.[102] "I was suspicious of the statements contained in Dr. Hadley's letter from the first," said Mrs. Evans. "We tried in vain to get information about the burial of the body in Puerto Rico."

Sue Hadley's family received another letter from Amos Hadley, written from Texas on January 2, 1919, in which he expressed a desire to tell about Sue's death in detail. He was suffering from grief, Hadley said, "and so broken up that he thought he'd 'never attempt to practice medicine again.'"[103] Disgusted, Hadley's brother-in-law said that he was in contact with the Richmond police and added prophetically, "We will do all in our power to locate Dr. Hadley and turn him over to the authorities."[104]

The letter to Sue Hadley's family, like discarding his wife's personal effects, was one of a series of actions by Amos Hadley that seemed to invite suspicion and investigation. After his wife disappeared, Hadley went to the jewelry store of D. Buchannan & Son at 225 West Broad Street and had the diamond from a woman's ring reset in a man's setting. Sue Hadley was still wearing her black kid gloves when she was found, and the fact that the left one had been torn indicated that someone removed them from her before throwing her in the James.[105] The story of the diamond ring revived the theory that jewelry "had been torn from the dead woman's left hand by her slayer," noted an observer. Again and again, Hadley committed blunders in his escape from Richmond. He was always described as an intelligent man, but things like blatantly signaling to Mrs. Evans that his wife was not returning to their home gave a cold-blooded practicality to his actions and indifference about how they might appear to even casual examination.

Events surrounding the sensational crime moved quickly. While the fugitive doctor was being sought in Texas, Sue Hadley's sister traveled to Richmond to positively identify the body of her sister, arriving on January 29, 1919. She was described as "prostrated" by her experience in the morgue.[106] Dr. James Whitfield, who served as coroner and "City Chemist," continued his exploration of Sue Hadley's stomach to discover the exact cause of her death. Dr. Whitfield said that he had removed Sue Hadley's skull and was analyzing her brain tissue. A late report came in stating that her fugitive husband had been spotted in Pearland, Texas, but a newspaper in the Texas town of Paris assured readers that Hadley had been seen at his mother's home in Friendswood as late as January 23.[107] Going one better, the *Corpus Christi Caller-Times* ran the headline "Two Hadleys Arrested," reporting the arrest of men answering the description of the missing doctor at two different Texas border towns on the night of January 26.[108]

Days went by with no news of Hadley's whereabouts, but Sue Hadley's family in Cincinnati were determined that her killer would not escape justice. "Negotiations are under way, it was learned today, with a view to having the Pinkertons join the hunt for Dr. Wilmer Amos Hadley," stated a Baltimore newspaper. "It is stated that the family will spare no expense in its efforts to run the fugitive down."[109] The Pinkerton National Detective Agency was established in the 1850s, had gained some fame as an intelligence source for the Lincoln administration in the Civil War and then made a specialty of hunting train robbers in the late 1800s. In the early twentieth century, the detective agency became known for strike breaking, but Pinkertons, with their famous motto "We Never Sleep," were the logical resort when local law enforcement failed to produce results in a fugitive case like Hadley's. The Evans family was wealthy enough to fund any amount of investigations, agents and transportation necessary to capture their daughter's killer, and they let it be known that they would "spare no expense in its efforts to run the fugitive down."[110]

By February, there was still no word of Hadley's capture, but the city that bore the shock of his crime was braced for his eventual return. "With practically all their evidence assembled and a strong circumstantial case against the fugitive physician, Henrico County officials are now devoting their energies toward the capture of the former army surgeon."[111] Despite that, and even with the extensive network of Pinkerton men on the case, no word arrived of an arrest. Sue Hadley's headless, dissected corpse was still in Fulton in August 1919 at Nelsen's Funeral Home. Since no exact cause of death had been determined, the body was still held by the Henrico coroner over the protests of Sue Hadley's family in Cincinnati.[112]

The big headline in Richmond on September 2, 1921, described a mine war going on in Logan, West Virginia, and there was a call to use federal troops to quell the armed unrest during a vicious coal strike. Army troops in New Jersey were preparing to go to the coal fields to settle what had turned into a shooting war.[113] As important as that headline was, it shared the same font as the news of the capture of Amos Hadley by the Pinkerton Detective Agency in New Mexico. After receiving a telegram from Pinkerton with news of its capture of Hadley, Henrico sheriff Sydnor and the county's Commonwealth attorney, W.W. Beverly, packed their bags and boarded the train for Denver, Colorado.[114]

Hadley's road back to Henrico County began with Richmond police chief C.A. Sherry receiving a phone call from an unnamed "prominent Richmond business man" who, in turn, had a friend who said that Hadley was living in disguise on a remote ranch in northern New Mexico near the Navaho Nation. A Pinkerton man was dispatched undercover and managed to meet the rancher, who said that his name was Westwood and confirmed it was Hadley. The man once described as "the dapper little doctor" dressed in a "clerical" manner had a weathered appearance with a shaven head and a long, bushy beard.[115]

According to the manager of the Pinkerton office in Richmond, J.W. Erb, the agent, didn't want to arrest Hadley in New Mexico, where the fugitive may have had friends who would come to his aid. Instead, the Pinkerton man managed to talk Hadley into an automobile trip in Colorado.[116] Once across the border, the unnamed agent confronted the doctor, who freely admitted his identity and expressed a willingness to return to Richmond. "Pinkerton operatives reported he had allowed his beard to grow a foot long, and his garb was quite ministerial in appearance. He spread the report he had gone there to recover from tuberculous and was tanned a deep brown."[117]

Perhaps the harsh and solitary life on the edge of the New Mexico desert finally exhausted Hadley, or he was once again simply unable to calculate the consequences of his actions. The Pinkerton agent found Hadley a very different fugitive from his usual quarry and was impressed by the doctor's impassive attitude. "He declines to comment on the case," reported the detective, "and appears to be undisturbed by his arrest."[118]

As Hadley and his escort were working their way back to Virginia, Richmond was rocked on the morning of September 6 by headlines saying that Hadley confessed to murder before the prisoner left Denver. "It is said that, when the physician saw the great mass of evidence that Henrico County officers, with the aid of Pinkerton detectives, had obtained against him, he broke down and in a husky voice admitted his guilt."[119] "I have come across some hard cases in my twenty years of experience in this game," said Erb, the Pinkerton man, "but this confession reveals the most gruesome, sordid crime I could imagine."[120]

On the morning of September 7, 1921, the Henrico sheriff and Commonwealth's attorney departed Chicago with their prisoner, but not before telegraphing the text of Hadley's confession to authorities back in Richmond. Broad details of the killing of Sue Hadley began to appear in print, and as the facts of the murder were recalled and readers of the *Times-Dispatch* were reminded, "The crime which resulted in the death of Mrs. Hadley for sheer atrociousness and extreme coldbloodedness, the Henrico authorities believe to be almost without precedent."[121]

According to Hadley's confession, his nemesis, a Dr. Griffith, had a history of paying too much attention to Sue Hadley, and this seemed to be some kind of vague foundation of a defense plea. He said that Dr. Griffith had been hounding him ever since Hadley practiced medicine and that "Dr. Hadley later quarreled with Dr. Griffith, the latter learning that Hadley had acted indiscreetly with a nurse at the hospital." Later, in Redcliff, Colorado, Griffith appeared again and then followed Hadley to Tennessee, where Hadley maintained he saw him talking to Hadley's wife. Griffith allegedly appeared in Charlotte, North Carolina, and followed the Hadleys to Richmond, and Hadley's confession included "a long list of 'persecutions' at the hands of both Dr. Griffith and 'my wife.'"[122]

The introduction of a "Dr. Griffith" into the story mystified the authorities in both Henrico County and the city of Richmond. Local death records were examined and private physicians interviewed, but no one knew of Dr. Griffith and there were no missing persons by that name. No Dr. Griffith was ever associated with Westhampton Hospital. Mr. Erb of the Pinkerton agency, quite familiar with tales told by criminals, said that he thought Dr. Griffith may have been invented by Hadley "to excuse the killing of his wife by some account of attentions to Mrs. Hadley by Dr. Griffith." Another theory was that the shooting of Dr. Griffith that same afternoon was the foundation of an insanity defense by Hadley and his only chance of avoiding the electric chair. Since Hadley's capture, authorities had to concede that "his actions [seem] to have been rather peculiar at times."[123]

In his confession, Hadley said that as he and his wife neared the Westham Bridge in their canoe that fateful afternoon, he came fully prepared for what happened next:

> *When we got near there, I told her we would take a drink of whiskey. I made her drink first. The whiskey contained chloral. She soon became unconscious. I took the anchor of the canoe, which was a large rock, and tying it to her body, I dropped the body overboard. There was a man sitting in the bushes along the shore who I recognized as Dr. Griffith, and I drew my revolver and shot him.*[124]

"He stated that he was enraged beyond all control by these attentions and murdered them both, throwing her body in the James River," but he failed to explain what happened to the body of Dr. Griffith.[125]

The men traveling with Hadley on the trip across the country found the accused murderer oddly indifferent to the gravity of his position, and Hadley was reported to be in a fine frame of mind and sleeping well on the way back to Richmond. "He has a good appetite and read most of the way back from Denver. The trio arrived in Richmond on the morning of September 7, and when questioned by the press said only, 'I have no statement to make tonight. I have communicated with my father, C.J. Hadley, of Friendswood, Texas, and I am awaiting his arrival before I employ council or make a statement.'"[126]

Hadley was taken from Main Street Station to the old Henrico County Jail, which still stands at 2117 East Main Street. While there, the mystery of "Dr. Griffith" was cleared up with a telegram from a Dr. J.A. Griffith of Hollywood, California. The real Dr. Griffith wired Henrico sheriff Sydnor that he had worked with Hadley briefly in a hospital in Eagle, Colorado, for several months in 1916 but hadn't seen either Hadley or his wife since then. "It is said the two men did not get along well together, a fact manifest to all that knew them and all culminating with the account of Griffith suddenly appearing on the river bank as Hadley killed his wife were all a fabrication."

The actual Dr. Jessie Ansley Griffith, interviewed in his California home, called Hadley's story "the ravings of a madman or the diabolical desire of a guilty man to drag one innocent down for revenge....The real trouble started at the hospital when he tried to work an insurance company, pretending some sort of injury to his back. I exposed him, and that turned him sour against me."[127] Perhaps the appearance once again of Dr. Griffith on the banks of the river the very afternoon he killed his wife made perfect sense in Hadley's mind—a grand culmination of his problems being solved. Dr. Griffith was the imaginary embodiment of his past professional difficulties and affronts, while Sue Hadley was the impediment to what Hadley imagined was his future happiness.

"Hadley's claim that I was with his wife at the time of murder absolutely false," read Dr. Griffith's telegram.[128] Henrico officials thought with the truth about Dr. Griffith widely known, Hadley had little choice other than to simply plead guilty and face the consequences. He was said to have told Sheriff Sydnor, "I'll take my medicine like a man," and that is exactly what the Henrico authorities thought he would do.[129]

Hadley retreated even deeper to his indifference about his fate. "He is now in that mental frame of mind where he now no longer takes any interest in what is published about him, for he now refuses to read the newspapers." When Hadley said he didn't care what happened to him, a reporter said that the remark "is not attributable to a case of nerves, because he is holding up well, eating heartily and sleeping regularly, but that he is extremely lonesome and feel himself abandoned by both friends and relatives, he makes no effort to conceal."[130] The only thing that seemed to penetrate through Hadley's phlegmatic defenses was a telegram from his father in Texas, who said he would be unable to travel to Richmond and made no assurance that he ever would. "Upon reading the telegram, Hadley displayed the only emotion he has shown since he was locked up in Henrico Jail. He quickly regained his composure, however, and resumed reading a magazine."[131]

By the beginning of October, a grand jury in the matter of the death of Sue Hadley had been convened, as Hadley calmly whiled the day away in the Henrico jail. "Hadley appeared as unperturbed when he was taken into the courtroom to hear the date of his trial read as when he played solitaire in his lonely cell." Hadley's newly hired lawyers, State Senator Julian Gunn and T. Gray Haddon, said that they would not seek an examination for mental competency for their client.[132]

The trial of Dr. Wilmer Amos Hadley for the murder of his wife began at 10:00 a.m., October 25, 1921. People involved in the tragedy arrived in Richmond, like Sheriff Wynn of San Juan County, New Mexico, who came to testify as to the circumstances of Hadley's arrest. The mother of the accused, Mrs. C.J. Hadley, arrived from Texas to attend the trial of her son. From Brooklyn came Hadley's former lover, Gladys Mercer, now married and known as Gladys Zobell.[133] One of the Commonwealth's most important witnesses would not be available to testify: Mrs. E.G. Evans, his West Grace Street landlady, died the night Hadley was arrested in Colorado.[134]

The courtroom at the Henrico Courthouse was packed with people wanting to see the famous Dr. Hadley. When the trial began, it immediately became apparent that Hadley himself was completely oblivious to the proceedings that would decide his fate. As he stood for the plea, "He betrayed no incidences of nervousness, nor did he, at any time, display any indication of interest in what the clerk was saying." Asked how he pleaded, he said in a loud and clear voice, "Not guilty."[135]

Mrs. Zobell, Hadley's former fiancée, was described as "very pale and nervous" as she took her place on the witness stand. She maintained her composure while answering questions from prosecution attorney W.W. Beverly but withered under questioning by the defense. Within a few minutes, she was weeping bitterly and had to be escorted to the juror's room, where she was attended by Dr. J. Fulmer Bright, the Henrico coroner. The prosecutor read letters from Hadley to Gladys, often referring to their future together on his Texas ranch. Many were signed by Hadley, "Lots and lots and lots and lots of love." Gladys Zobell, having collected herself, returned to the courtroom with her attitude changed and defiant. She was married in January 1920, she told Hadley's attorney, and did not divulge her husband's name or occupation, saying that it should not be dragged into the already wrenching proceedings. Some questions she simply refused to answer.[136]

Besides the humiliating correspondence she had exchanged with Hadley, filled with breathtaking lies and betrayal, Gladys Zobell was asked about an engagement ring that the accused had given her in anticipation of their marriage, and she produced it. She also still had the watch Hadley had given to her, the one with the Christmas inscription of "Gladys, may all the coming years be as bright." There was one horrific detail: inside the watch were the initials S.T.H., those of the watch's previous owner, Sue Tinsley Hadley.[137]

Hadley's appalling detachment from his trial and his apparent lack of either compassion or humanity left the spectators in the courtroom perplexed and dismayed. "Dr. Hadley appeared to be the most unconcerned man in the courtroom all during the day, watched the young woman to whom, at one time, he had engaged himself, to be married very closely, as she answered questions, but without the slightest sign of emotion, although he was apparently more interested in what she had to say than he was in what any of the other witnesses had to divulge....Hadley looked straight at her, a smile sometimes playing about his lips."[138]

Most damning was the confession that Hadley had signed in Colorado. Sheriff Webb Snydor was called to the stand and gave an overview of the pursuit of Hadley and his arrest, until the point that he mentioned a "volunteer statement" made by the fugitive. An argument broke out between opposing council as to the admissibility of the document, and Judge R. Carter Scott had the jury removed from the room. After some debate, Hadley's confession was admitted to evidence. In the document, Hadley recounted killing his wife and "Dr. Griffith" the same afternoon, although it omitted the names of anyone who might have assisted him when he fled Richmond.[139]

This confession sealed Hadley's fate, and by the following evening, all the evidence had been presented and all the witnesses had testified. By 5:00 p.m. on October 26, the jury had returned from its deliberations. The scene at the Henrico Courthouse and the accused were described at that moment: "The courtroom was packed when the jury returned a verdict of 'guilty of murder in the first degree' and the coolest man who heard the verdict was the man on trial for his life—Dr. Hadley."[140] Defense attorney Gray Haddon immediately filed a motion for a new trial, using the somewhat circular logic that if Hadley had indeed committed the murder, "he could not possibly be normal, and was, therefore, entitled to be treated with that leniency accorded to those not considered entirely sane." Hadley, ever cool and collected, turned to his attorneys and said, "I wish you gentlemen to understand that I am more than appreciative of the services you have rendered me. There was not a flaw in the defense." One reporter watched as Hadley, with his fixed expression, was taken back to the Henrico jail. "The doctor smiled as he was being led to his cell."[141]

Hadley returned to the same courtroom on October 27 to hear Judge Scott deliver his sentence. He stood as the clerk of the court asked solemnly, "What, if aught, have you to say?" Hadley replied in a husky voice, "I have nothing further to say then that all the facts in this case will never be known." Judge Scott looked down at Hadley and told him that he would be electrocuted on December 9. His sentence concluded with the dread words, "And may Almighty God have mercy on your soul." Hadley resumed his seat beside his lawyers, "folding his arms across his chest and exhibiting no indication of whatever disturbing thoughts, if any, he was entertaining." Hadley's chilling indifference to his impending death was not just for public consumption but rather was ingrained throughout his behavior, with his jailors noting that after his sentencing, the doctor still "ate the regular prison fare with apparent relish last night, and after the lights were turned out retired to his bunk and was soon asleep."

Hadley fell from the public eye during the period between his trial and the December 9 execution date, spending his days reading in his cell and apparently completely resigned to his fate. He asked his lawyers to drop any appeal, requesting that he not be forced to go through with another trial. Only intervention by Virginia governor Westmoreland Davis could save Hadley at this point. But the day before the execution, Davis said that he saw no reason to intervene in the case and that the doctor's electrocution would proceed as scheduled.[142]

Before dawn on December 9, twelve witnesses assembled in the dark at the gate of the Virginia Penitentiary in Richmond. They were quietly ushered into a room where twelve chairs sat in a semicircle facing the electric chair. The chair itself combined the familiar form of a large oak armchair with the foreboding addition of its straps and wiring and sat by itself on a wooden base beside a large grounding point built into the concrete floor. Two prison guards stood by, but their help was not needed as Hadley walked into the "death chamber" with a steady stride at 8:00 a.m. At 8:07 a.m., after two surges of electricity through his body, Hadley was pronounced dead. Hadley's spiritual advisor and fellow Quaker, Justice J. Hoge Ricks, took charge of the body, and it was sent to the L.T. Christian Funeral Home at Boulevard and Park Avenue. The Hadley family was expected to return the body to Pearland, Texas, Hadley's former home.[143]

Instead, however, Hadley's gravestone can be found in among the thousands at Richmond's Hollywood Cemetery. He was buried the day after his electrocution in a plot owned by the Richmond Society of Friends, a faith that, by tradition, disdains grave markers. Contrary to that practice, Hadley's grave is marked, but his small tombstone is oddly engraved with only his initials and the years of his birth and death. The inscription "The Lord Is My Shepherd" seems almost like a banal addition in the face of the glaringly truncated identification. Amid the richly marked tombs of thousands of Richmonders, the granite obelisks and marble mausoleums, Haley's solitary marker appears inscribed to be deliberately dim and then forever lose the memory of the man in the grave. Why it is marked at all (none of the other five burials in the same plot is marked), contrary to Quaker custom, is a mystery.[144]

Perhaps down by the Kanawha Canal, at that intersection of Old Westham Road and Old Bridge Lane, is where the echoes of the lost lives

The grave marker for Amos Hadley at Richmond's Hollywood Cemetery. *Author's photo.*

of the philandering doctor and his ill-fated wife can still be heard. There beside the little bridge over the canal, you can almost see the gentleman in his army trench coat and the lady in the tan raincoat. They stand there as they wait, unable to talk to each other over the roar of the passing coal train. Imagine that tiny, crystalline moment when Sue Hadley slid her arm in her husband's and drew him close, recorded then and recalled a century after it took place. Now it can be seen clearly as the embodiment of the relationship between these two doomed people: a warm and loving gesture returned with deceit and implacable malevolence. Theirs is a story told in that instant. Even now, after one hundred years, we can only wonder at such an incredibly heartless betrayal of the cruelly deceived victim, murdered in midstream on the James.

Chapter 4

DEATH, DESIRE AND THE DIVORCÉE

A FAMILY MAN'S FATAL AFFAIR

R ichmond has always famously clung to its past, and its idealized history defined its race and society, while oversized monuments to Confederate generals and leaders rose above the skyline. Nevertheless, by the late 1920s, fueled by a roaring economy, Richmond was clearly changing and moving away from its traditional sleepy southern mindset. The city was bustling, and major buildings were being constructed all over town, like a new hotel, later named after Richmond's own John Marshall, and the wonderfully elaborate auditorium the Shriners were building on Monroe Park called The Mosque. The "Movietone" process was being installed in the Capitol Theater, reportedly only the sixth instance of the new technology in the world. "The possibilities of this innovation are said to be almost unbelievable," gushed one Richmond newspaper, astonished by the Movietone's synchronized sound and picture.[145] In keeping with its ambitions for the city, the Richmond Chamber of Commerce searched for a man they characterized as "a full-time, high-powered, big-caliber, executive manager"[146] to head a national advertising campaign to promote the city's growing potential.

This was precisely the kind of man the Hermitage Country Club was looking for as well. Founded in 1900, in 1925 the club was seeking a new secretary to manage the facility. It wanted a discreet and rock-solid man with the right grit who could maintain the quiet aquifer of money and privilege just below the immaculate grounds of the club. The secretary was supposed to respond to any breach of club decorum, manage member relations and

John Wesley Faison, family man and murderer. *Author's collection.*

attend to the club's finances. Among the other duties of the post were to deposit any funds collected during the average day and during tournaments. This required the secretary to frequently carry a pistol for protection.

The Hermitage Country Club found just such a solid man in John Wesley Faison. Born in Richmond in 1896, Faison was an upright citizen, father of five children, Sunday school superintendent and faithful husband. He was a former handwriting instructor at Richmond's John Marshall High School, indicative of his disciplined and methodical nature. Married at nineteen and a deacon in the Baptist Church, Faison lived a quiet life with his family on Cliff Avenue in Richmond's North Side until the age of thirty-one.

In the summer and fall of 1927, all hell broke loose in Faison's otherwise orderly life in the form of Elsie Snipes, a Richmond music teacher who lived in a second-floor apartment on Hanover Avenue. Later, Faison recalled meeting Snipes, who immediately cooed, "Gee, but I like you" in his ear and kissed him. "I was so infatuated with her, soon after our meeting, that I forgot everything else. To me she was the one supreme ideal among womanhood."[147]

To say that his life was derailed by this encounter hardly describes how Faison almost immediately threw over everything he once held dear, beginning with his marriage to his wife, Martha. Faison told her that he was in love with the most amazing woman—and it certainly wasn't Martha. Their five children, ages one to twelve, must have looked on with anguish as Faison shoved past their mother and out the door of the family home. He left for Elsie Snipes's apartment and sometimes didn't come home for days, going on what Faison called "honeymoons" with Snipes to Petersburg.[148] "Mrs. Snipes undertook to vamp Faison and by July 7, she had him in her power," Faison's lawyer described the relationship. By September, the lawyer said, Snipes had told Faison that she was pregnant.[149]

Snipes was slightly older than Faison and was perfect to play the role of *femme fatale*. But unlike Faison, Snipes's life was unfettered by family or commitment, as (for reasons never stated) her former husband was raising their two children in North Carolina. Faison later described his time with Snipes as an "ultra-Bohemian life," keeping Snipes in whiskey while still financially supporting his stunned family.[150]

One of the more remarkable elements of the story of Faison was that his obsession with Snipes occurred with the full knowledge of his long-suffering wife. The *Times-Dispatch* termed Martha Faison a "plain and sad-faced woman"[151] who, when she talked about the effect Snipes had on her husband, said, "He called her the most wonderful girl in the world."[152]

The memory of who her husband had been and her Catholic faith apparently sustained Martha Faison through the emotional hurricane that had been her marriage. A reporter attempted to untangle the unusual situation for his readers: "Mrs. Faison took the attitude that the alleged intimacy between her husband and Mrs. Snipes might soon come

Elsie Snipes, the *femme fatale* in Wesley Faison's life. *Author's collection.*

to an end and in consequence be forgotten. Therefore, for the sake of appearances, cordiality between the two women appeared to exist."[153] In the end, Martha Faison proved a far better player of what proved to be a volatile contest between the two women.

That volatility is evident in the letters Faison sent Snipes, filled with sentimentality in some letters but ferocious jealousy in others. "My dear little wife, I am a slave to your beautiful self," he wrote on one occasion to Snipes. But when Faison felt that there might be another man in her life, he was brimming with rage. "I am so jealous that somehow I think my mind will crack," Faison wrote to Snipes in a letter found by police. "Here I am in hell when I thought I was in heaven. I know it is another man. Damn his soul, I would tear him limb by limb. It is all for me or not at all. If this occurs again, I will not be responsible for what happens."[154]

On the evening of November 15, 1927, Elsie Snipes was entertaining friends at her apartment. Her guests were Mason Smith, Mrs. Minnie Wade and Snipes's chiropractor, Dr. Robert Bybee. Wade had been invited to dinner at Snipes's apartment that evening. Dr. Bybee got a call to come over, and Smith tagged along. Despite arriving at different times, the three guests were all of one mind when it was time to depart. Snipes told them that Faison had telephoned her several times, and perhaps knowing better than to be there when the mercurial Faison arrived, they got their coats on to leave. Snipes begged to go with them as they piled out the door, and later in court, Dr. Bybee was asked, "What conversation took place between you and Mrs. Snipes when you left?" "I just said," Bybee recalled, "that we had stayed too long already."[155]

Her guests said that Snipes came down to the street to their parked car to plead for a ride, telling them fearfully, "Don't leave me here—Faison is coming back." Told there was no room in the automobile for an extra passenger, Snipes's parting words to them were "You'll be sorry you left me" before her friends drove off down Hanover Avenue.[156]

Faison appeared at 3131 Hanover soon after Snipes's guests departed, leaving just the two of them in the apartment. According to Faison, as he and Snipes talked, she left and went into the bedroom to make a telephone call. Faison's description of his actions before the gunshot sound like those of a blasé sophisticate in a silent movie: "She went into the bedroom and shut the door. I lit a cigarette….I looked at the pictures on the walls; I played a tune with one finger on the piano; I looked at some photograph records and while I was looking at the records I heard the explosion. I did not know what it was. I called to Mrs. Snipes and she did not answer, I went into the bedroom then saw her in a chair with a hole in her forehead."[157]

Semiconscious, Snipes sat slumped in a chair in the bedroom with a bullet hole through her right eyebrow, her eyeball having been forced from the socket by the pressure of the impact of the bullet on her skull. The projectile had gone completely through her head at a downward angle, exiting the base of the brain, hitting the floor behind her and ricocheting into the woodwork of a nearby bed.[158] Bessie Wright, who occupied the apartment above that of Mrs. Snipes, later testified that she heard a gunshot and then a man called out, "God! I have killed Elsie: I have killed poor Elsie. What am I going to do? May God have mercy on my soul!" Footsteps were heard going down the hall and outside, then back into the apartment again and out into the street.

Across Hanover Avenue, Charles Ford was awakened by a commotion. He looked out and saw a man come out of Snipes's apartment building, pace around the corner into Cleveland Street, go back inside 3131 Hanover and then appear again carrying a woman in his arms.[159]

The newspaper accounts the next day stated, "Faison, the 31-year-old manager of the Hermitage Golf Club, came into Stuart Circle Hospital at 1:15 A.M. November 16, with the body of a ninety-eight-pound woman over his shoulder." Visibly distraught, Faison told Dr. E.N. Pleasants, who was on staff that morning, "My God, doctor, she is the only woman I have ever loved." Faison knelt beside her gurney whispering words of encouragement to the dying Snipes, who mumbled something incoherent in reply.[160]

The doorway of 3131 Hanover Avenue, where the frantic Faison emerged carrying the bloody body of Elsie Snipes. *Author's photo.*

Martha Faison arrived at the hospital within minutes of Faison, having been telephoned, she said, from Snipes's house by her husband after the shooting. Remarkably, Mrs. Faison told police (and later testified under oath) that she'd been on the phone with Snipes just before she was shot.

According to Martha Faison, Snipes told her that she didn't want to break up the Faison household and would "destroy herself" instead. Elsie Snipes died at eight o'clock on the morning of November 16, her death certificate noting the cause as "gunshot wound—whether suicidal or homicidal cannot be determined at this time."[161]

On the morning of November 21, after cutting the telephone wires to the house, Richmond police surrounded Faison's father's home on Seminary Avenue, banged on the door and arrested John Faison on a charge of murder.[162] Readers of Richmond newspapers (and certainly members of the Hermitage Country Club) were astonished to read that this pillar of society and a man known for his righteous and upright manner stood accused of such a scandalous crime.

The sensational nature of Snipes's murder began to get national attention from news services. A newspaper in Burbank, California, ran a photo of the murder scene, "Clubman" Faison and "pretty divorcee" Snipes, in contrast to a prim headline in a Clinton, Illinois newspaper that simply characterized the tortured relationship between Faison and Snipes as "Man Held in Death of Sweetheart."[163] Even the American Communist Party newspaper, the *Daily Worker*, picked up the story. Under the headline "Murdered Woman's Diary Indicts Many," the paper assured its readers that Snipes kept a diary of her "dealings with the wealthy clubmen."[164] This was echoed by a Richmond paper, which ominously reported, "Mrs. Elsie Holt Snipes' diary, containing references to many prominent Richmond men, looms as a ghost in the trial of John W. Faison, charged with murdering Mrs. Snipes, gets under way this morning in Hustings Court."[165]

Martha Faison made an appeal to the membership of Hermitage Country Club and raised $1,400 toward Faison's $10,000 bond, the remainder of which was put up by unnamed wealthy friends and Faison's parents.[166] The arrangement of bail for Faison was a routine procedure, but the unconventional nature of the relationship between him, his wife and Elsie Snipes remained almost more than the Richmond newspapers were able to explain. One thing was clear: the perversion of a marriage with five children that was completely undermined by a woman who might be described in the slang of the day as "fast" was utterly unpalatable in Richmond. The fact that she was killed in the course of such reprehensible behavior might have been seen by many in Richmond as poetic justice for North Carolina libertines. These things happen.

In an attempt to report on the trial of Faison, Richmond's newspapers tried to navigate some of the grittier elements of the testimony in order

Martha Branch Faison. *Author's collection.*

to spare the sensibilities of their readers. The rumor that Snipes may have been pregnant and that this may have been the cause of Faison's rage was treated gently by the *Times-Dispatch*, which obliquely described the autopsy findings this way: "No trace of the alleged delicate condition of Mrs. Snipes was found." In contrast, the same newspaper tittered, "Some portions of [Snipes's] 1927 diary, make spicy reading," although that content was never disclosed in court.[167]

Faison's trial commenced on December 12, 1927, and was followed avidly by Richmonders. Even though Richmond was rocked by the murder trial of Thomas Pollard only a few years before, it was still said of the Faison trial that "no case tried in recent years has had a stronger grip on the public imagination."[168] The Faison trial was made even more salacious by the admission into evidence of the letters Faison wrote to Snipes, letters in which he tells her, "I still feel the warmth of your sweet kisses on my lips." Perhaps most tellingly, Faison also wrote to Snipes, "I am unreasonably jealous of you."[169]

That degree of "unreasonable" jealously came through clearly in letters that echoed the obsessive quality of Faison's attachment to Snipes as well as his capability for violence. "I can picture you with somebody else when you should be with me. I wish to God he could die the most horrible death and I would watch and laugh. I would tear him limb from limb."[170] Another letter on Hermitage Country Club stationery said, "You are my ideal. I just want to worship your dear sweet face all the time....I know you will be true and come back to the one who waits for you. Am signing off now through station LOVE." He signed the note, "HUBBY WESLEY."

Perhaps nothing was more vivid for the jury and spectators at Faison's trial than the testimony of Bessie Smith, who lived in the apartment above Elsie Snipes. "Miss Smith made a splendid witness. Her manner was straightforward, and the tone in which she repeated the phrases she heard early on the fatal morning were dramatic." Miss Smith was also unshakable in her recollection of hearing a gunshot and then a man's voice crying out, "God, God, I've killed poor Elsie! Lord have mercy on my poor soul. What will I do?"[171]

Using this dramatic testimony, the Commonwealth built its case that Faison, driven with the same fervor that drove him to abandon his family, fell into an equivalent white-hot rage and shot Snipes through the head with a .38-caliber revolver, which he brought to her apartment the night of the murder. The Richmond city coroner, Dr. J. M. Whitfield, testified that it was unusual for a suicidal person to shoot themselves in the face with a gun by holding it at arm's length and pulling the trigger with a thumb. The lack of powder burns on Elsie Snipes's forehead was also an important piece of evidence. Snipes was a small woman, and even at arm's length, the six-inch-barreled revolver would have put the muzzle that much closer to her head and subsequently left powder burns.[172]

The path of the bullet that drove through Snipes's head was a critical part of the prosecution's argument. Harold Colley, a North Carolina lawyer hired by Snipes's family to assist with the prosecution, emphasized this point by using the actual chair and pieces of Snipes's bed in a demonstration in the courtroom. The wound was consistent with Snipes being shot by someone standing in front of her, Colley said, someone like Faison, angerly confronting her from the bedroom doorway with a revolver in hand. Colley's address to the jury became so intense that Martha Faison's sister, Mrs. Y.A. Baldwin, fainted and had to be lugged out of the courtroom by family members during Colley's accusation of her brother-in-law.[173] Colley thundered:

> *Could she sit on this chair (bringing out the chair on which the woman is said to have been seated), hold the telephone, the receiver and this pistol all at the same time and then while in that position could she shoot herself? Look, look at the angle at which that bullet would have to go. She couldn't hit her head, with the index figure on the trigger. She would have to hold it way up like this (demonstrating his theory)....About the time the Hermitage Club found out about his affair and he sees he's about to lose his position. He found out she didn't have the big music class he thought she had. He schemed how to get rid of her.*[174]

In contrast to this scene of murderous rage, his defense attorney presented the picture of a completely rational Faison, who said that night he calmly informed Snipes that he was leaving her and going back to his family. He then described puttering about Snipes's apartment while she made a call until he was startled by the sound of a shot. "I called Mrs. Faison as soon as I heard the shot in the bedroom," is what Faison recalled at trial, "telling her that Elsie had shot herself." It was only after that conversation with his wife that Faison loaded the wounded woman in his car and drove her to Stuart Circle Hospital. Martha Faison arrived minutes later. In court, the entirety of that conversation of that frantic phone call between Faison and his wife was not revealed, a phone call that took place as Elsie Snipes lay dying.[175]

Lawyer W.R. Widenburg spoke for Faison, portraying his client as having been led astray and deluded. At the same time, Elsie Snipes's character flaws became an essential part of the defense:

> *I tell you gentlemen that when a woman indulges in immorality it is because the image of God has passed from her mind. When this woman realized disaster…what did she do? She roamed around and finally landed in Virginia. She wasn't fit for motherhood. She landed at Mrs. Gilham's boarding house and got thrown out of there. I won't say how bad she was, but the poor fool* [Faison] *thought she was the finest woman in the world—and she was to him.*[176]

The Faison trial ran for seven days, at the end of which the jury foreman reported, "We are hopelessly divided." A mistrial was declared on December 21, and Faison posted bail and left to spend Christmas with his family. "We are not going to stop fighting," Martha Faison said with a rare smile as she and her husband left the courtroom. Faison's fate was deferred until the 1928 docket of the Hustings Court.[177]

It would be March 1928 before Faison was back at Richmond City Hall in the Hustings courtroom, testifying on his own behalf in front of another jury. He endured a full hour of cross-examination from Commonwealth's Attorney Dave E. Satterfield. "Reciting his story in a voice pleasant and nicely modulated," Faison steadfastly related the story as he explained it in his first trial. One reporter observed that Faison "maintained a perfect composure throughout the cross examination and told the story of his elicit [*sic*] relationship with Mrs. Snipes without apparent shame or discomfort."[178]

The coroner, Dr. Whitfield, was recalled to the stand to testify once again on the improbability that Snipes was able to commit suicide. He said that in his long experience, someone shooting themselves never held the gun so as to be looking down the barrel when it went off, as the defense maintained. The powder traces on Snipes's face were consistent with the revolver being some distance from her when it went off.[179] Whitfield's testimony, combined with the trajectory of the bullet through Snipes's head, presented the chilling picture of Elsie Snipes sitting in the "death chair" and looking directly into the muzzle of the revolver held by Faison, standing at the door of the room. The last thing she saw was the flash of the gun going off, with her lover's face behind it.

The ever-faithful Martha Faison testified again, dragging her humiliating role in her husband's philandering into the light of the courtroom. "Oh, yes, I knew Mrs. Snipes and I knew what was going on—Wesley never lied to me—but I just kept hoping and praying he would awaken to the call of his family and return to being the same good husband and father he was before meeting Mrs. Snipes."[180] Martha Faison also stuck to the original story that Elsie Snipes told her that she would "destroy herself" only seconds before she was shot in the head.

No matter how earnest his explanations and how calm his demeanor, the jurors didn't believe Faison, nor did they believe Martha Faison's story of her conversation on the phone with Snipes. On March 20, the jury debated six hours before returning a verdict of guilty—but of voluntary manslaughter, not murder. The crime of voluntary manslaughter, explained the *Times-Dispatch* for its readers, "Is indicative that Faison killed Mrs. Snipes in the heat of anger and without malice or premeditation." The jury set the penalty, and the judge prepared to announce the sentence. "Faison stood, hands in trouser pockets, rocking back and forth slightly on heel and toe: he was calm, and apparently well satisfied with the verdict."[181] Faison's reaction when the verdict was announced was described in this way: "[H]is expression contorted into what seemed remorse; his lips compressed; and then…a few minutes later, to the suggestion of a smile."[182]

Throughout both trials, Faison stoutly maintained that he would appeal his case if he was sentenced to "so much as a day in jail." Despite that, he accepted his sentence for manslaughter, knowing that with time served he would be in prison for only eight months. An appeal at this point could result in a far more severe sentence. Faison decided not to press his luck and quietly accepted the verdict and light penalty.[183] At the end of the trial, Judge Wells told Faison:

> *This jury has, in my opinion, been exceedingly lenient and I trust this will be appreciated by you when you complete your term in the penitentiary.… When you are permitted to take up your life again, to return to the exemplary conduct which characterized your early career; return to your life and family with a better outlook on life and, in consequence, make a man of yourself.*[184]

The sentence of a year in jail was unprecedented, but in the eyes of the Richmond jury, the truly guilty party had already been punished. Elsie Snipes—alcoholic, failed mother, homewrecker and seductress—had already been brought to justice, and she and her destructive behavior had been put to an end at the hands of a morally superior man who simply had a momentary and perhaps justifiable lapse of control. Considering that he could have received decades in jail or even the death penalty, the slap on the wrist Faison received was a statement that loose women leading good men astray would not be tolerated in Richmond. Maybe the men of the jury saw in themselves the same vulnerability to seduction and derailment. Perhaps there was the same tiny flicker of weakness in each face around the jury table.

There were some in Richmond who were appalled at what they felt was the worst miscarriage of justice in Richmond in decades. His light sentence of a year for the crime of manslaughter in the Faison trial was too outrageous for even the *Times-Dispatch*, where an editorial appeared on March 22 under the title "Crime and Punishment." "A man if found guilty of killing a woman and is sentenced to one year in the penitentiary. A Negro woman is given thirty years for forgeries amount in the aggregate to some $70. A Negro steals a ham and is put away for five years or ten. What is wrong with us?… If [Faison] was guilty—and the jury reported that he was guilty—sentencing him to serve until October 12 for his crime is the most astounding action ever taken by a Richmond jury."[185] John Mitchell Jr., editor of Richmond's African American newspaper, the *Richmond Planet*, impressed by this rare call for judicial parity and fairness, reprinted that editorial on the front page of the *Planet* the following week.[186]

A *Times-Dispatch* reader named Arthur Weston agreed that the sentence given Faison was ridiculous and wrote to the editor on April 2, "Elsie Snipes is dead. John Wesley Faison stands convicted of killing her. His punishment, considerably less than a year means a most stupendous liar and a murderer will soon gain his liberty to return to an exemplary life."[187] Faison himself, while still maintaining his innocence, confidently announced his intention to revert to "a higher life" just as Judge Wells instructed. Faison told the press, "My life before this unfortunate affair speaks for itself, and I am determined to again tread that straight and narrow path that leads along the road of upright living and good citizenship."[188] Faison said goodbye to his family (including Martha, who was now pregnant) and was transferred from the Richmond City Jail to the Virginia State Penitentiary on March 31, 1928.[189]

With the credit for the time he spent in the Richmond jail, John Wesley Faison was released on October 29, 1928, after just thirty weeks in the penitentiary for the murder of Elsie Snipes. He was greeted by his family, including the infant who was born while he was in prison.[190] With every encounter with the press, he repeated his noble resolve to keep to the straight and narrow, and Faison apparently did just that. He led a remarkably conventional life, moving his family to Salisbury, Maryland, and converting from the Baptist Church to Catholicism. Faison retired after working thirty-five years for the Delmarva Power and Light Company, was active in his church and joined the Knights of Columbus. When he died in 1972 after a long illness, his obituary in the Salisbury newspaper recounted that Faison once taught at John Marshall High School in Richmond but tellingly neglected to mention anything about being secretary of the Hermitage Country Club.[191]

His wife, Martha, who stayed the course so faithfully through her husband's trial, died of a stroke in 1984 at the age of ninety-two and was survived by five children, twenty grandchildren and twelve great-grandchildren.[192] How many of those children knew that their grandfather or great-grandfather was a convicted murderer and that their grandmother or great-grandmother was complicit in the murder as well? She twice lied under oath that Snipes had assured her of her intention to kill herself to save the Faison household, supposedly just seconds before the gunshot. Perhaps John and Martha Faison never again spoke of their lives back in Richmond, the city where he once abandoned his family in a frenzy of infatuation and lust, killed his lover in cold blood and avoided the electric chair with the help of Martha's perjured testimony.

Perhaps the two children of Elsie Snipes never knew that their mother was shot through the head and murdered by a married man with whom she was having a torrid love affair and in death had been judged by the Richmond press as debauched and amoral. Snipes had been examined through the ethical lens of the city of Richmond and was punished for her excesses; her killer was protected by the sanctimonious attitudes of a city secure in its moral superiority.

Chapter 5

SODOM ON THE JAMES

MURDER AT RPI

Today, 712 West Franklin Street is the address of a high-rise VCU dormitory called Webster S. Rhodes Hall, but sixty years ago, a brick home typical of that once-fashionable part of Richmond once stood on the same spot. The house, constructed in the late 1880s by one of Richmond's Scott families, was a mashup of projecting bays and heavy window framing, combined with elaborate belts of decoration. Like so many Franklin Street properties, the house was sold to Richmond Professional Institute (now Virginia Commonwealth University), which converted the house at 712 West Franklin into the school's first dorm for men in 1949.[193]

Bloody murder arrived at the house on West Franklin in the unlikely form of a slender, dark-haired young man who climbed the steps to the second floor on the evening of May 7, 1956. Alfred Vischio Jr. had come to see his nineteen-year-old friend James Edward Whitlow, who was a freshman at RPI and Vischio's former roommate. It had been almost eighty degrees that day, but Vischio was nevertheless neatly dressed in a suit and tie, which concealed a five-shot .38-caliber Smith & Wesson revolver in a holster under his jacket.

A native of Brooklyn, New York, Alfred Vischio entered the U.S. Navy in July 1952 but was admitted to the naval hospital in Portsmouth, New Hampshire, after suffering a nervous breakdown. He was honorably discharged from the navy in October 1953 for medical reasons. Vischio later said that he was interested in coming to Richmond and attending RPI because of its distributive education classes and then later switched his major to sociology.

Vischio was a junior at RPI when he alarmed fellow students by brandishing a gun and threatening to shoot himself.[194] Other students disarmed Vischio, who subsequently withdrew from classes in mid-March 1956. Vischio's military service made him eligible for treatment at Richmond's McGuire Military Hospital. Authorities at the hospital said that Vischio attempted suicide "at least once" but helpfully added, "[B]ut he never tried to harm anyone else."[195] He was discharged one month later and told to return to his mother's home in New York to recover. Vischio came back to Richmond on October 6, rented a room on Grove Avenue and spent the eighth looking for a job before meeting his pal Jim Whitlow that evening.[196]

In contrast to the urbane Vischio, Jim Whitlow was a country boy from the tiny town of Clover, near the North Carolina border. After graduating from Halifax County High School, Whitlow attended rural Bridgewater College in the Shenandoah Valley.[197] For some reason, Whitlow chose to transfer to RPI, perhaps to experience the big-city life in Richmond. He entered a medical technician program at RPI and told friends that he hoped to one day be a pharmacist.[198] Interviewed later, other students in the dorm told reporters that Whitlow and Vischio became good friends since Whitlow had started classes at RPI in September.[199] The two had been in separate rooms but moved in together by September 22. They spent a holiday in Florida and then went to Brooklyn and spent Christmas in Vischio's home.[200]

Monday morning, May 7, 1956, RPI dean of students Dr. Margaret Johnson received a call from a man named W. Glaus Coker of the 2400 block of Grove Avenue. He told Johnson that "Al Vischio" had come to Richmond and was staying with Coker, an old acquaintance. He was concerned because Vischio received a gun in the mail while at Croker's house. Vischio told him that it was just for target practice; however, Coker was uneasy and wanted Dr. Johnson to tell him the circumstances that led to Vischio leaving school the previous March. Johnson told Coker that for privacy reasons, a committee would have to meet before she could comment on Vischio and his actions.[201]

While the appropriate committee was being assembled, RPI administration contacted McGuire Hospital and located the psychiatrist who had last examined Vischio to inform him that his former patient was back in Richmond and reported to have a gun. When told the situation, the doctor responded that even though Vischio had attempted suicide on more than one occasion, he did not feel that he was a danger to anyone else. Dr. James Cottrell, the manager of the hospital, later said, "At the time of the boy's discharge from the hospital, there was nothing to suggest he might be dangerous to himself, and there had never been any reason to believe he might be dangerous to others." The RPI committee determined that since Vischio was not a student, there was nothing the school could do except tell him to stay out of the dorms. Nevertheless, William O'Connell Jr. (who knew Vischio and had given him a ride to McGuire Hospital back in March) called Richard Burnette, the dormitory manager for 712 West Franklin, to tell him that Vischio was back in town. If he showed up at the dorm, O'Connell told Burnette, do nothing to upset him but call O'Connell immediately.[202]

Burnette enlisted two other students, and all three kept a lookout on West Franklin Street for Vischio. Whitlow came in, and they asked him if he knew Vischio was back in Richmond. Whitlow said he had just seen Vischio over in the cafeteria. While at the dining hall, Vischio ran into Dean Johnson. She told Vischio that she didn't think he should stay around campus, as it might not be beneficial to his recovery. He responded that he wanted to be with his friends, and the two agreed to meet at Johnson's office the next day.[203] Dorm manager Burnette and his two volunteers briskly walked the two blocks to where they thought Vischio was still eating in the dining hall and therefore just missed the nicely dressed if agitated young man when he came through the gates of 712, up the steps and into the dorm.[204]

We have only Vischio's version of the next few minutes, as told to the police in chillingly matter-of-fact tones. He went to Whitlow's room, and the two talked about mail that Vischio was having forwarded to him from the West Franklin address. In the course of relating his conversation, Vischio made an odd aside. "He said he felt sorry," Vischio said of Whitlow, and he mused, "I don't know what he meant by that."[205] Whitlow said that he was tired and was going to take a nap, going to bed and setting his alarm clock for 7:00 p.m.

Vischio left Whitlow at that point, went to another room and chatted for a few minutes with a student, who then left. Vischio said he picked up a copy of *Life* magazine and leafed through it for a while, then stood up and returned to the bedroom where Whitlow was asleep with his face to the wall. "'As soon as I came back in the room, I pulled the gun out and just did it," said Vischio, snapping his fingers, "just like that." Thinking about it a minute, Vischio added with a tone of wonder, "I never fired a pistol before in my life before."[206]

Whatever happened, the reality was that Alfred Vischio went to Whitlow's bed, bent down and emptied his five-shot revolver into the back of his friend's head. The detonations must have been deafening in the small room, with

Alfred Vischio is bundled into a police van on the grounds of McGuire Veterans Hospital, having just been arrested for murder. *Author's collection.*

the unmoving Whitlow's wavy dark hair and the sheets around him concussing at every shot as he lay face down on the bed. RPI student Charles Stewart was upstairs on the telephone when he heard what he thought were firecrackers. Slamming down the phone, Stewart and Joe Moore were the first ones to enter Whitlow's room to see what was going on.[207] "A blanket was over his head; we pulled it back and saw what happened…as I remember it, I think there were four or five shots." Whitlow's death certificate says he died at 6:50 p.m., and presumably the alarm set earlier in the evening went off beside his now blood-soaked bed ten minutes later.[208]

Alfred Vischio's ears must have been still ringing from the five gunshots when he walked down the stairs of the house on West Franklin and out the front door. Standing by the gate on the sidewalk was Peter Miles of Louisa County, Virginia, who knew Vischio well. Miles said Vischio asked him for a ride up to the home of Dean Johnson, who lived on Grove Avenue. Miles took one look at Vischio and said, "I told him I didn't know where the Dean lived and he walked off." Miles described Vischio as looking wild, saying, "His eyes were as big as your fists." Vischio hurriedly turned west on West Franklin for two blocks and then north on Shafer Street to Broad Street. There he hailed a cab to take him to McGuire Veterans Hospital.[209]

It would be interesting to know what was going on in Alfred Vischio's mind as he rode in the cab toward McGuire, the unaccustomed weight of the now-reloaded Smith & Wesson still on his belt and his mind racing. At 7:45 p.m. that evening, a guard on duty at McGuire Hospital named Sterling Monk was surprised to see a slender young man on the grounds listlessly walking toward him carrying a revolver. He reached down and took the gun from Vischio's limp hand. When asked what he was doing, Vischio replied in a monotone voice that he "shot a man at 712 West Franklin." Monk escorted Vischio to the hospital admissions office, where the police were summoned. Vischio was arrested on the spot and transported downtown.[210]

Reporters flocked to the city jail after the news of the sensational killing spread. Vischio said he didn't know why he shot Whitlow. "I'm sorry," said

Vischio, "It's the worst thing that could have happened. I wish I could cry, but I can't."[211] The *News Leader* quoted Vischio on the front page: "I don't care what happens. All they can do is send me to the electric chair." Later, he added, "The detectives think I'm hard because I don't show much emotion. But I've always been that way. I always keep everything to myself. Doctors have told me that was one of my troubles."[212] Under ordinary circumstances, the young killer might have generated some sympathy for his mental state, but his utterly impassive and nihilistic attitude added a thrill of horror to the inexplicable murder and fueled much speculation about the two young men involved.

These early interviews in the newspapers are where the first implications of homosexuality about Vischio are seen, and by association, Whitlow's orientation was also called into question. The *Richmond News Leader* described Vischio: "The youth is about 5 feet, three inches tall, and weighs about 115 pounds" and "rumpled and unshaven after a night at the first police station." The newspaper's reporter added archly, "His large dark eyes and hands that are manicured like a woman's draw attention."[213] Peter Miles, who encountered Vischio on the way out of the dorm seconds after the shooting, told authorities that "Vischio was very jealous of Whitlow. He would become angry and upset if Jim went with anyone else to eat at the cafeteria."[214] This was one of several implications that the death of Whitlow may have been the result of jealous rage between lovers, and rumors roared around the RPI campus. Detective Sergeant F.S. Wakefield said that Vischio signed a statement in police custody admitting that he killed Whitlow but refused to say why, lending an air of deeper mystery to how the two young men felt about each other.[215]

Further complicating theories about the relationship between Vischio and Whitlow was the newspaper story that ran on May 12, 1956, about a girl who attempted suicide in a Shafer Street RPI dorm. "The girl's father yesterday confirmed that she had attempted to kill herself about April 15th. She is under psychiatric care at Medical College Hospital." Vischio told the police that the unnamed girl and Whitlow had been dating and that Whitlow had tried to see her three days before he died.[216] Because of the discretion of the Richmond press, nothing more appeared in print regarding this incident. Still, the story of the girl and Whitlow is an interesting sidebar and had to have complicated the already fraught relationship between Vischio and Whitlow.

Dr. Harry Brick was a psychologist from the nearby Virginia State Penitentiary who examined Vischio soon after he was arrested. He described Vischio as a man of "dull intelligence—a day dreaming and emotionally flattened individual" with an IQ of 87.[217] Dr. Brick labeled Vischio as a "homosexual and potentially suicidal individual" and said that Vischio "admitted to episodic depressions as well as day-dreaming such as being 'champion of the world'—a big dancer and going to the electric chair."[218] Brick recommended that Vischio should have a thorough psychiatric evaluation. At the order of the Richmond Hustings Court, Vischio was sent to Southwestern State Hospital, a state facility in Marion, Virginia.[219] By early November, Vischio had been tested and pronounced sane "with no evidence he had been psychotic in the past" by a panel of doctors and was back in Richmond, with his trial set for the twenty-seventh.[220]

After further delays, the Richmond Hustings Court got 1957 off to a sensational start when Vischio's trial for the murder of Jim Whitlow began on January 2, 1957. Since the accused had already signed a statement indicating his guilt, "Indications were that the Vischio trial is expected to consume little time."[221]

The *Richmond News Leader* reported that the process had taken less than two hours before "Alfred Vischio, Jr., who once day-dreamed about going to the electric chair, was sentenced to life imprisonment instead." After the defendant's emotionless plea of "guilty," Judge Moscoe Huntley recommended that Vischio be ineligible for parole, meaning only a pardon from the governor could free him from a life spent entirely in the Virginia State Penitentiary. Watching their impassive son were Vischio's divorced parents, and his mother sobbed aloud as the clerk read the sentence. Also in the courtroom was the family of Jim Whitlow, looking at their son's murderer. Newspapers repeated the telling quotation from Vischio when he miserably explained that he was unusually close to Whitlow "because he taught me to dance." Before he was led from the courtroom, Vischio was briefly interviewed, and the "neatly dressed" murderer expressed his dismay with the sentence of "natural life" without the possibility of parole. "Beyond that," he said impassively, "there is not much else I can say."[222]

In the meantime, the leadership of RPI was scrambling to defuse any implication that they had been negligent when they learned that Vischio had a gun in his possession and was on campus. RPI defended itself by saying that Vischio had committed no act that justified calling the police and having him arrested. In the report issued by RPI, the specter of homosexual relationships between students arose but was dealt with by a fog of veiled references, code words and euphemisms.

All that remains of the former RPI dorm at 712 West Franklin Street is the decorative fence along the street. This is where the wild-eyed Vischio met Peter Miles seconds after shooting Whitlow. *Author's photo.*

The school's report spoke of "alleged practices," but Alvin Chandler, president of the College of William and Mary, did not explain what these practices were. The college in Williamsburg was then the parent school to RPI and controlled the policies and procedures of its satellite college in Richmond. Chandler said little other than there would be new guidelines to "cover the complete field of student discipline." The RPI report also primly noted that they could not find any "direct evidence of an immoral nature involving students, facility members, or persons connected with Richmond Professional Institute." The investigating committee implied that more careful screening at the school might eliminate some of the obviously gay applicants on campus such as Vischio, with his tell-tale neatly manicured hands and tidy appearance that verged on effeminate. If the school was guilty of anything, the report said, it was not more closely supervising student activities and allowing rumors of the "alleged activities" to persist. Improved screening, Chandler seemed to be saying, was all that was needed to keep problematic applicants like murderous homosexuals from admission.[223]

RPI's student newspaper, the *Prescript*, quickly responded with an editorial that questioned the allegiance of any student objecting to the way the Vischio case was handled and tidied up. "The school has struggled for many years trying to build a strong and vigorous college finally to see this effort go down the drain when students make careless remarks damning their school," intoned an editorial soon after the murder on West Franklin Street.[224] "No student should be enrolled here if they can't stand behind the school," added Tom Monahan, president of the Student Government Association at RPI. The author of an editorial in the student newspaper agreed, adding darkly that RPI could well do without "disloyal" students who apparently felt that Vischio and Whitlow were far more than college chums and it was that very real relationship that resulted in tragedy.[225]

One year after Whitlow's death, an editorial in the *Richmond News Leader* claimed that RPI teemed with "young blood and radical professors" and coyly acknowledged that the Whitlow murder involved an element of homosexuality. In an editorial titled "RPI Is a Help Where It Is," the *News Leader*'s editor's sly choice of words left even the most naïve Richmonder able to understand: "Persistent rumors of immoral student behavior were climaxed last year by the queer circumstances of the Vischio homicide case."[226] The subject of homosexuality on the RPI campus was always hovering just out of sight, kept in the shadows by official disavowal, oblique references and crafty innuendo. The murder of Jim Whitlow momentarily brought gay lives and gay relationships to the attention of students and faculty, and both groups immediately and publicly disavowed such "alleged activities."

Alfred Vischio Jr. served his sentence in the Virginia State Penitentiary on Belvidere Street, just a mile away from the scene of his murder of Whitlow. At some point, he won release, left Virginia and died in Massachusetts at age seventy-two in 2007. His obituary noted that he was survived by "a dear friend, Dr. John T. Woodland of Maine," so perhaps Vischio finally found the sympathy and support he so badly needed after the trauma of his crime and the subsequent years in prison.[227] As a Korean War–era veteran, Vischio qualified for a grave at the Massachusetts National Cemetery in Bourne, where he is buried under a government-issue veteran's tombstone that simply notes his rank as seaman and the dates of his birth and death. In contrast, Whitlow's grave in Clover, Virginia, has the stern epitaph "Prepare for Death and Follow Me." The choice of words is perhaps emblematic of disapproving parents who may have felt that they made a horrid mistake when they allowed their innocent son to go to school in Richmond and fall prey to the big city—a veritable Sodom on the James.

Today, almost no one remembers the shock that ran through the RPI student body with the news of the shooting of Jim Whitlow by Alfred Vischio. The victim has been in his rural grave more than sixty years, and the house that was their dorm is long gone. The old bedroom that once contained such an unimaginable scene of coldblooded murder has been erased as though its brick walls never existed. Only the cast-iron fence from the former house at 712 West Franklin remains at the address. There, at the gate, is where Peter Miles met the wild-eyed Alfred Vischio as he emerged from the dormitory seconds after shooting his friend upstairs. With the passage of six decades, there are fewer and fewer old RPI students who remember that day of bloody rage, jealousy and madness in a Franklin Street dorm that once cost two young men their lives.

Chapter 6

THE MURDER OF PATROLMAN JOHN A. TIBBS

UNSOLVED AFTER EIGHTY YEARS

I play poker on Friday nights at a house near the James River, and among the players is a retired Richmond policeman. I happened to ask him one evening if he was familiar with the murder of a patrolman on Broad Street in the 1940s. "Sure. Tibbs. Everybody has heard of that." He looked out the window briefly at the river and turned back to me with a small, rueful smile. "Everybody always said it was another cop that shot him."

More than eighty years have passed since the murder of Patrolman John A. Tibbs, who was killed in a store on Richmond's Broad Street on October 20, 1940. Ostensibly, the facts are as stark as the black-and-white flash photos a police photographer took of the scene: a uniformed policeman lay inside the back door of a vacant store at 721 West Broad Street, his skull fractured from a blow to the back of his head. In the center of his forehead between his eyes was a neat bullet hole surrounded by powder burns. He lay stretched out on his back, his unfired service revolver near one hand and his flashlight beside the other. A loose pile of bricks at the scene seemed to tell a story: burglars, interrupted while trying to dig through the wall into an adjoining store, were surprised at their work and ambushed the veteran cop.

Patrolman Tibbs's assignment was to monitor a section of downtown Richmond on foot. In his case, it was an area bordered by Broad Street on the north, Main Street on the south, Harrison Street on the west and Adams Street on the east—an area largely occupied by Virginia Commonwealth University today. This was not a beat without violence. Only three years before, another patrolman named William Snead was killed by a burglar on the sidewalk in front of 120 East Broad when the officer interrupted the robbery of a jewelry store. The robber managed to wrestle Snead's service revolver from him and shoot the policeman through the head before being wounded and arrested by other officers.[228]

In 1935, a small article in the *Times-Dispatch* recounted Tibbs finding the front window of a gas station at Madison and Grace Streets shattered and the business looted.[229] At 3:00 a.m. on a May morning in 1936, Tibbs discovered a burglary at 815 West Broad Street, where someone entered a finance company and robbed its safe of $1,100.[230] Another memorable watch in 1938 was spent controlling the crowd that gathered at a fire in the Dr Pepper Bottling Company plant on Linden between Cary and Main, where Tibbs and one other policeman kept order until reinforcements arrived.[231] Lost kids, sleeping drunks, car accidents and domestic disputes were all things Tibbs encountered on his rounds—sometimes enforcing, sometimes arbitrating. No matter what, as his commanding officer emphasized on more than one occasion, Tibbs was "absolutely fearless, and always on the alert."[232]

Tibbs began his last watch at 4:00 p.m. on the evening of October 20, 1940, as he left the Second Police Station, crossed Broad Street and strode off toward his beat. It was the cool day where the highs only reached into the sixties. As Tibbs walked down Grace Street, the scenes around him must have seemed as familiar as those in his own home. He had been a cop for fourteen years, much of it on the same beat, seeing the same faces in the store windows and on the front porches he passed. The steady presence of the congenial Tibbs must have been a comfort to Richmonders who spotted him and often chatted with the officer.

Patrolman John A. Tibbs. This portrait hangs at the Richmond Police Academy with those of other Richmond police officers who died in the line of duty. *Author's photo.*

Tibbs was certainly a familiar figure to the woman in the ticket booth of the Lee Theater (today's VCU Grace Street Theater) at 934 West Grace Street.[233] She glanced up and saw him around 4:45 p.m. as he walked through the glare of the lights of the marquee overhead that advertised the Bing Crosby musical *Rhythm on the River*, which was playing that weekend.[234] Part of Tibbs's routine was to check in at various call boxes along his beat at designated times, signaling to his precinct station that all was well. Tibbs didn't call in that evening as he should have at 5:00 p.m. and then did not call at 7:00 p.m. either. That is when the captain in charge of Second Station sent out Lieutenant Gray Miller and Sergeant Paul in search of Tibbs.[235]

Eventually, there were thirty policemen and seventy civilian volunteers combing the area that night, checking backyards, alleys and doorways for the missing policeman. It wasn't until after midnight that Tibbs's fellow patrolmen J.V. Hanes and A.W. Gorman noticed that the door at the rear of the business at 721 West Broad Street was ajar. Seeing that it appeared to have been forced open, they swung it back and cautiously stepped inside. John Tibbs's body was on his back on the floor in the brick dust, arms outstretched. By his right hand lay his service revolver. Near his left hand was his flashlight, the switch in the off position. A neat bullet hole was between his eyes.[236] When Detective Lieutenant Dan Duling arrived on the scene, he bent down and examined Tibbs's service revolver and noted that it was completely loaded and unfired.[237]

Beside Tibbs's body was a pile of bricks that had been recently dug from the wall of the building. On the other side of that wall was the Zeeman Clothing Company, which was said to have done $7,000 worth of business the day before. Presumably, Tibbs surprised the burglars, who were determined to dig their way through the wall, bring the Zeeman safe into the vacant building at 721 West Broad and then break into it without setting off any alarms in the clothing store. Unfortunately, whoever was breaking through the wall was unaware that Zeeman's did not have a safe at all and there was no money on the premises.[238] A bad plan turned into a worse one when complicated by the murder of a policeman, and a simple charge of attempted burglary changed in an instant to a crime with the death penalty—but only if the killers could be caught.

The readers of the *Richmond Times-Dispatch* were pummeled with bad news on the morning of October 21, 1940. German bombers were appearing over London nightly in the bombing campaign called the Blitz, while U-boats were wreaking havoc in the North Atlantic, with dozens of ships lost in a single night. Locally, the news was just as depressing. Workers at local Selective Service boards were preparing to post the first lists outside The Mosque (today's Altria Theater) of young men to be called up for the new military draft. A local grocer, Robert Smith, was attacked in his store on the now vanished Washington Street—he was bludgeoned to death and

Policeman W.G. Edwards inspects the door at the rear of 721 West Broad Street that Tibbs discovered just before he was murdered. *From the* Richmond Times-Dispatch.

had his throat cut the previous evening. Joining all this horrific news was the somber image of John Tibbs, staring out of his official police department photograph, accompanied by the story of his sudden death and the hunt for his killers.[239]

On North Twenty-Third Street, the news of Tibbs's murder arrived in the middle of the night—a night burned into the memory of his daughter, Jenny. Sixty-two years later, she recalled:

> *I remember waking up—it was a Sunday when it happened. And I remember waking up during the night and hearing Momma talking to one of our neighbors in the other room. She woke us up the next morning, and she said, "I need to tell you something." My sister and I were sharing a double bed, and I was sleeping on the side where Momma was sitting when I woke up. She was sitting there crying when I woke up. And she said, "Somebody's killed our Daddy." And I'll never forget that.*[240]

By the next day, the man who murdered grocer Robert Smith in his store had been identified and arrested, but there were no developments to report in the Tibbs case. Positioned on the front page beside the accounts of the two murders was an article that three high-ranking members of the police department were suddenly fired; in the words of the chief of police, they were "dismissed for the good of the service."[241] This seems unfortunate timing for the police department—an agency, according to Mayor Gordon Ambler, whose morale was "at a very low ebb," now made even worse by a cop killer being at large.[242]

Despite that lack of confidence as a department, all Richmond police officers who were not on duty came to Tibbs's memorial service at Woody's Funeral Home. A crowd crammed into the chapel, and half the seats were taken by uniformed cops. In attendance were Mayor Ambler, the chief of police and practically all the city government and council. After the ceremony, the mourners drove out to Oakwood Cemetery, where Tibbs's grave is marked by a tombstone proudly noting his status as a Richmond policeman and his badge number, 113.[243]

In the weeks and months that followed, there was scant progress in the investigation into Tibbs's murder. Instead, Richmond's attention turned to the treatment afforded the wives and families of policemen killed in the line of duty. The press trumpeted the sad truth that Tibbs's widow, Namaah, and their five young children would receive a paltry $70 per month support—and that only for a year. Members of the police department passed the hat

Richmond police officers examine the bloodstained area where Patrolman Tibbs's body was found. *From the* Richmond Times-Dispatch.

and raised $750 for the family, but that was the extent of their support. The poignant story of this large family in distress and the resulting outrage that the police were treated so shabbily caused an outpouring of donations. One man who chipped in $5 toward a fund set up for the Tibbs family called it a "shame" for his city: "[S]hame for a city that will allow its men to give their lives without making some adequate provision for those he is apt to leave behind him."[244] Mrs. Pauline Butts wrote to the *News Leader*, urging the police be paid more and that more be hired. "Had there been more police than we have, Policeman Tibbs would not have been killed," she wrote to the editor of the *Times-Dispatch*, "and I hope they get the man or men who did it and put them in the chair."[245] Many Richmonders, whether driven by embarrassment or pity, contributed to an account established for Tibbs's wife and children, and a benefit concert was performed at The Mosque for the memorial fund.[246]

In March 1942, the City of Richmond agreed to allocate $2,500 to the Tibbs family, to be added to the $4,900 raised by contributions from citizens and fellow police.[247] After that, there was very little said about the murder of Patrolman Tibbs except for a small memorial notice in the newspaper on every anniversary of his death, a sad little reminder of a crushing loss, simply signed, "Wife and Children."[248] The death of John Tibbs was a terrible blow for his family, and Jenny Tibbs Van Volkum sadly recalled the effect of her father's murder on his family and her mother's broken heart. She said, "The way it was left with us—I was nine years old, and mother was never able to talk about it and until the day she died—she was ninety-four and a half when she died in 1998—she hoped it never opened up again because she could just not deal with it."[249]

Always hovering in the background of the story of John Tibbs is something even darker than his apparent ambush and coldblooded murder. These were occurrences so oddly menacing that they were burned into a child's memory and would be recalled vividly seventy years later:

> But one thing I remember. When he was home one day—I guess in the morning—a car pulled out in front of the house. He looked out, and he told Momma, "They're coming here, and I am going in the bedroom and you tell them I'm not here." Well, two or three men got out, and I don't remember exactly but they had on hats and overcoats, dressed nice, and they came to the door and asked for Daddy. And she told them he wasn't there, and they asked when would he be back and she said she didn't know, that he had to go to work or whatever. And after they left, Daddy came out of the bedroom, and she said, "What was that all about?" And he said, "Don't worry about it. They just want me to do something that I'm not going to do." Well, that was all I remember about that. See, like I said, I was nine years old, so there could have been a lot going on that I didn't know.[250]

She also remembered her father's book, a small memo book he kept with him while on patrol. The question of what became of this little item is another disquieting memory for Tibbs's daughter:

> He had this little book, a little pocketbook, that he kept in his pocket with notes, and he always told Momma that if anything ever happened that he wanted the chief to get that book—to make sure he got that book. And I don't know how long it was, but a few days after things settled down this man I was telling you about [a supposed friend of Tibbs's] told Momma that the chief had sent him to get the book and she gave it to him. The next day, somebody else came from the chief's office to get the book.

Now, that is as much as I heard about that. So, I don't know what ever happened about that or what ever happened to that book.[251]

These memories are unsettling and hint of other, unseen influences at work in the fate of Patrolman Tibbs. The most frightening element is the rumor, passed down from generation to generation of Richmond cops, that Tibbs was killed by another policeman. Unlike so many of the fallen officers who died in the line of duty in Richmond over the decades, Tibbs's name is still familiar, and Debbie Blanchard, Tibbs's granddaughter, said, "Every police officer that I've talked to knows who he is, and he died in 1940."[252] Years have passed and hundreds of men and women have graduated from the Richmond Police Academy, but Tibbs remains like a ghost story told at night around the squad room to rookies, a frightening tale now eighty years old. The persistence of this story of possible betrayal and the decades-old legend of a uniformed traitor among Richmond cops is itself noteworthy.

An intriguing detail from the police photos of Tibbs's body hints at some kind of treachery and a killing far beyond that of a simple ambush at 721 West Broad Street. Tibbs's was an era when Richmond Police Department uniforms included a duty belt with cartridge loops to carry spare ammunition for the .38-caliber revolvers the police were issued. Looking closely at a crime scene photograph of Tibbs, stretched out on the floor at the rear of the store on Broad Street, a glaring detail is evident: on his otherwise full cartridge belt, there is one empty cartridge loop and a bullet is missing.[253]

This begs the question: who, that October night, needed a spare bullet and would stoop down and slide a cartridge from Tibbs's belt? It is doubtful that a conscientious, veteran officer like Tibbs would not be wearing a full cartridge belt for the inevitable inspection at his precinct, both before and after his shift. (Who would need to *not* come back to the end of watch inspection missing a bullet from his own belt or his service weapon?) The coroner said that one of the causes of Tibbs's death was a fractured skull; he was apparently struck on the head and knocked down. Why was it necessary that the unconscious patrolman be so brutally executed? Had the killer been recognized by Tibbs? What was said and what decisions were made in that time between Tibbs being knocked to the ground and the deafening roar of that pistol in that small space? Whose hand held that gun, a hand so determined and careful as to hold a pistol almost touching Tibbs's face and shoot him precisely and surgically between the eyes?

Tibbs, described by his chief as "always on the alert," was an experienced officer and not for the first time was cautiously approaching a darkened

The graves of Richmond policeman John Tibbs and his wife at Richmond's Oakwood Cemetery. *Author's photo.*

doorway by himself, gun in one hand and flashlight in the other. Perhaps he found a welcoming and familiar voice inside, relaxing after the tension of entering a dangerous space and letting down his guard until stunned by a blow to back of his head. Perhaps in the last moment of his life, Tibbs recognized someone in that shadowy hallway, someone he had arrested or someone he knew. Questions persist, and the Richmond Police Department is still, even after eighty years, not releasing any information.

In 2012, the *Richmond Times-Dispatch* ran an article about a service for fallen Richmond officers that described the extensive case file on the Tibbs murder, which included a forensic evidence report that was compiled by the Federal Bureau of Investigation and signed by Director J. Edgar Hoover. In the article, Richmond police detective Amira Sleem stated, "It has always been believed that patrolman Tibbs was killed by his own firearm, and the evidence at the scene supports that."[254] This is in direct contrast to the examination of the revolver on the scene in 1940 by Detective Duling, who was quite specific when he stated that the gun was fully loaded and "unfired." In 2011, Lieutenant Emmett Williams instructed Detective

Sleem to reorganize the forensic file so it could be "better used to train homicide detectives."[255] Williams maintained that the still-unsolved murder of Patrolman Tibbs "is certainly a case we could use as a training tool for future detectives to sharpen their skills."[256] Sharper detective skills have been needed in this case for decades, as no one has ever been prosecuted for the murder of John Tibbs. Instead, his life and the circumstances around his violent death in the line of duty all have been reduced to a teaching aid for the Richmond Police Department.

Despite that, the police will not open the Tibbs file to the public since it is still considered, decades later, an "open" case. A request under the Freedom of Information Act to see the Tibbs material was filed with the Richmond Police Department in 2020. All that was forthcoming were illegible photocopies of three newspaper articles concerning Tibbs and a copy of a 1940 reward notice. All notes, interviews, photographs and the extensive FBI forensic report were not made available, as the police department stated that "all other records will not be released because they are part of the criminal investigative file."[257]

There will be no justice and no peace for John Tibbs's family, as the facts about his death remain unknown, eighty years after the event. As Tibbs's daughter glumly said of the secrecy that surrounds her father's death, "I can't see the point. If these guys were still on the street killing people, it would be different. But they're all gone. They're all dead."[258]

The peculiar occurrences around the Tibbs murder, the patrolman's missing memo book, the apparent threats to the officer and his unsolved murder all demand resolution. While this could have been a simple criminal ambush, our city's police personnel believe that a cop, a hardworking family man just as many are themselves, was once executed by a fellow officer. The story persists down through the decades, and with it, a cry is still heard across eighty years of Richmond history for justice for Patrolman John A. Tibbs.

Chapter 7

VIOLET MERRYMAN

A YOUNG WOMAN GONE ASTRAY

In the spring of 1920, functionaries of the federal government began to move through Richmond's shaded streets, crooked alleys, wide boulevards and dirt roads to take the federal census. "Census enumerators have begun to make their presence felt in Richmond and to pry into every nook and corner of the city in their search for stray inhabitants," reported the *Times-Dispatch*.[259] Among those questioned by the census takers in south Richmond were two of the residents of a boardinghouse at 219 Cowardin Avenue: Effie Berry, an eighteen-year-old woman, and her sister, Violet, age fourteen, a girl with a distinctive misaligned eye. The sisters' workdays would have been filled with drudgery and routine, as each morning they made their way straight down Hull Street and into the heart of industrial Manchester. They both worked in Richmond's booming tobacco industry, Effie as an inspector in a cigarette factory and Violet as a cigar roller.[260] Across the river, downtown Richmond loomed against the sky with breathtakingly tall buildings, but except for some mills, Manchester was all low brick factories, belching smokestacks, cheap frame houses and everywhere the pervasive smell of leaf tobacco.

The Berry sisters probably worked in a large room of identically aproned girls, each bent over their tasks at a long table lined with chairs. This work was tedious and dirty, and sitting all day in the damp heat of a Richmond summer among the ranks of the rows of toiling women endlessly rolling cigars with their hands, Violet Berry imagined a different life for herself. Her marriage to a Richmond bricklayer named Eugene Merriman in 1930 did

Violet Merryman consulting with her lawyer in a holding room at the Henrico County Jail. Note her eye condition that made her instantly recognizable to the authorities. *From the* Richmond Times-Dispatch.

not last long but perhaps provided Violet her ticket out of the dirty streets of Manchester and away from the interminable cigars.[261]

Actual Detective Stories of Women in Crime was a 1930s true crime magazine whose January 1938 issue featured the story of Violet Merryman's misadventures "in her own words." The article was ghost-written by Walden Snell, who also wrote for *Startling Detective Adventures*. Snell cleaned up Violet's written voice for her story to the point that the narrator of "I Turned in My Lover for Murder" hardly sounds like a girl with an elementary school education in the American South: "I was born and raised in Richmond, Virginia. Until I was 22 my life was usual, commonplace, no different from millions of others....Much against my parent's wishes, I married the man whose name I use now."[262] The fictional Violet melodramatically described a man named "Captain" Laban Howard she met after she separated from her husband. "It may have been that strange power he held over me for so long after," says Violet in words reminiscent of radio theater of the day; all that is missing from her narrative is the swelling organ music behind her as she breathlessly recalled "that piercing, almost hypnotizing look in his eyes that wakes me even now from a deep sleep and I find myself trembling and sobbing."[263]

Laban Howard, known as "The Captain." Howard's abuse of Violet Merryman led to his spending the rest of his life in the Virginia Penitentiary. *Actual Detective Stories of Women in Crime* (January 1938).

The reality of Violet Merryman's boyfriend, "Captain" Laban Howard, was that he looked exactly like what he was—a thuggish former convict and professional criminal, well known to Richmond authorities and who referred to himself as "Captain" by virtue of his once having piloted a tugboat. In 1935, Howard was released from the State Prison Farm along with his good friend Edward Hawkins.[264] Hawkins was a former Virginia state policeman who had been fired from the force after being sentenced to six years in prison for shooting a man in Gordonsville.[265] The relationship between the two old ex-cons Howard and Hawkins is hard to define, but the results were the first act of a very long drama combining poor choices, bad company and brutal murder.

The Violet Merryman in the magazine article is shocked when a catty acquaintance from back in the days when Violet "was running around so haphazardly," as her prim alter ego described it, told her that her boyfriend and his pal Ed Hawkins had done time in the pen. "Laban, my gentle Laban, an ex-convict!" exclaims the fictional Violet, absolutely scandalized and not believing a word of it. "The woman was crazy. I was determined to do justice to the person I loved by dismissing the words as preposterous."[266]

By then, the real Violet Merryman had a police record of her own of eight arrests for various misdemeanor crimes (probably solicitation), and given the circles that she ran in, she had to know that Laban Howard was quite a notorious figure in the Richmond area.[267] Violet's "gentle Laban" described himself as a liquor seller and numbers runner for a Richmond gambling operation.[268] Since his release from prison, Howard was labeled in the press as "a sinister figure in Richmond's underworld" and was known have been involved in several safe-cracking jobs.[269] It is easy to picture Howard lurking in the scruffy apartments, roadhouses, beer joints and back porches of a hot, Depression-era Richmond summer, but it would have been impossible for his girlfriend Violet to not to have known who she was running with.

Perhaps the reason Violet and Laban Howard moved from Richmond to a small log cabin on Falling Creek in Chesterfield County was to beat the heat of the summer of 1936—or, more likely, to make it harder to be found. Their domestic bliss in the cabin was interrupted when "less than a month after we began our life together, Ed Hawkins came to live with us." Violet's magazine article, despite its overheated and unbelievable prose, does furnish a useful timeline of what happened in that cabin and afterward. The magazine, perhaps suggesting something even more salacious, also hints at a relationship between Howard and Hawkins beyond cellmates. "Before that, I had not realized that Laban and Ed were intimate in any way at all. And Laban offered no reason for their close acquaintance," mused Violet for the benefit of the reader's imagination.[270]

Whatever the relationship between the two men, August 15, 1936, found Violet, Laban Howard and Ed Hawkins all at the Falling Creek cabin with Laban's son, Shelton, who was an overnight guest. Violet later described the evening as a "drinking party."[271] At 1:00 a.m., Violet heard Howard abruptly get up and cross the room, and according to her later testimony, he abruptly shot his friend Ed Hawkins twice as he lay in bed. The account in *Actual Detective* had Violet reeling melodramatically. "'Shelton!' I sobbed, 'What's happened? What's happened?'" "Mr. Hawkins!" he muttered, "Dad's just shot him!"[272] It was not for dramatic effect that Hawkins screamed and writhed on the bed in pain, shot through the stomach and spine and unable to move his legs.

The testimony by his son at Laban Howard's subsequent trial provides the clearest picture of the scene: the cabin room with the bottle-strewn table, the smell of stale cigarettes and a light haze of gun smoke in the air, the harsh light of naked bulbs revealing the stunned expression of Violet Merryman, the flushed and enraged face of Laban Howard and the wide-eyed horror

Ed Hawkins, former Virginia state policeman, ex-con, Laban Howard's good friend and murder victim. *Actual Detective Stories of Women in Crime* (January 1938).

on the face of Shelton Howard. On the bed in the middle of a scarlet stain creeping across the sheets under the forty-watt light, Ed Hawkins lay gasping. It was a lurid scene in blacks and reds, made even worse by Hawkins's piteous cries for help. "Dad, you've got to help him," the fictionalized Shelton Howard says, "He'll die if you don't get him a doctor." "A doctor!" Laban was scornful. "There won't be no doctors or cops around here.…Violet, get me a towel," growled Laban in the magazine account.[273] Violet produced the towel thinking that he was going to finally staunch his old friend's wounds, but instead Laban wrapped it purposefully around the head of a hammer and sent Violet and Shelton out of the room. When they returned, Hawkins's skull was bashed in, and the body on the bed was still and quiet.[274]

Violet later testified in court that Laban forced her and his son to roll up Hawkins's body in blankets and put it in the rumble seat of their car. They drove to a spot near Petersburg, where Hawkins's bloody body was tumbled out into a honeysuckle patch. Rapidly decaying in the heat of the Virginia summer, he was found five days later, but no identification of the dead man could be made. Ed Hawkins was buried an unmarked grave in a local potter's field in Prince George County.[275]

Although they were never married, by January 1937 Violet Merryman was still living with Laban Howard and listed among her siblings as "Mrs. Violet Howard" in her mother's obituary. We don't know if that was her choice or if Laban Howard insisted she use his name.[276] Later, she described herself as though in the grip of some diabolical power, both dependent on and afraid of the "Captain," but the end, it was Violet who determined the fate of her violent boyfriend and it was her testimony that would put him in jail until the day he died.

In March 1937, Laban Howard was suspected of involvement in several Richmond burglaries and was picked up by the police, but the cops were unable to make a case against him. Without criminal charges, the authorities couldn't hold him, but Justice Elben Folkes did the next best thing and gave Laban forty-eight hours to get out of Richmond. Unwisely still in the city two days after the deadline passed, Howard tried to persuade Violet to go with him, and when she refused to leave Richmond, he became enraged and beat her up in her apartment at 123 East Ninth Street. In retrospect, this was a terrible mistake. Somebody called the cops, and things rapidly went from bad to worse for Laban Howard.

Nursing both a black eye and years' worth of grudges, Violet filed a complaint against the "Captain" with the police, telling the detectives, "You'll never know what terrible things that man has done."[277] When Howard was once again brought before Justice Folkes, the judge was not impressed to find him still in Richmond and sentenced him to twelve months in the city jail for vagrancy. Folkes told Howard that since he seemed to like Richmond so much, "he could—in fact he must—stay here another year."[278] With Howard safely bundled off to jail, the detectives returned to Violet's remark about the "terrible things" Howard had done. Violet apparently reached her limit after the beating she received earlier and "suddenly blurted out her version of Hawkins' slaying," including the whole nightmarish night culminating with the trip to Petersburg with Hawkins's body rolled in blood-soaked blankets and mashed into the rumble seat of the car.[279]

Events moved quickly in the matter of Ed Hawkins's disappearance. As a result of Violet's story, the body in the pauper's grave outside Petersburg, with its bullet wounds and crushed skull, was exhumed and identified as Hawkins. Howard was served a warrant from Chesterfield County in his Richmond jail cell, charging him with Hawkins's murder, and the "Captain" claimed not only that was he innocent but also that he didn't even know his old friend Ed Hawkins was dead.[280] The dead man's brother and uncle came to Richmond from Rockingham County and collected the box of bones that had been Ed Hawkins, but the broken skull, with its distinctive dental work, was retained by Chesterfield County as evidence in Howard Laban's upcoming trial.[281]

Violet was also arrested by Chesterfield police and held in Richmond as a material witness. In the newspapers, she again bore the title of "the Merryman woman," a subtle signal by the press of an amoral female and used to describe any woman ranging from a flirt to an outright criminal.[282] Horace Berry, "the Merryman woman's night watchman father," said he gave up his attempts to raise the $2,500 bail for his daughter, so Violet would remain in a cell at Second Police Station. Howard's son, Shelton, was released from jail in Petersburg on bond and went home to Norfolk.[283]

Laban Howard spent his time in jail composing a lengthy letter to the public, "laboriously written in pencil on yellow paper." It followed the first statement in print by Shelton Howard describing the night his father murdered Ed Hawkins. "After reading this morning's paper, there is no doubt in my mind that my son, Shelton, is trying to protect himself and Violet," Howard wrote. His story of that night was that he had gone out to buy a case of beer, and when he returned, Shelton and Violet were there and Ed Hawkins was dead. Howard said, "They both looked like they were scared to death," which is probably the only true statement made by the "Captain" as he tried to pin the murder on his son and girlfriend.[284]

Violet's photograph, titled "State Witness," appeared in the *News Leader* on April 13, 1937, showed her smartly dressed and with a broad smile on her face as she entered Chesterfield Courthouse on the first day of the trial of Laban Howard for murder. "The petite, henna-haired woman-in-the-case flitted in and out of the clerk's office, posed for pictures, laughed happily and said she had gained 20 pounds since she unburdened herself to the police."[285]

While Violet may have been enjoying her time in the spotlight, the trial itself was described as lacking the high drama that might have been expected. The completely blasé manner with which the head of the hapless Ed Hawkins was handled is indicative of the lack of sensationism throughout the trial. Hawkins's skull, with the massive holes in each side, were impassively "handled by witness after witness with complete detachment." Mrs. Frances B. Wood, Hawkins's ex-wife, examined a dental plate and confirmed that it was Ed's, as it was helpfully fitted repeatedly in her former husband's skull, demonstrating it could only be Hawkins's. One witness, after fiddling with the jaw bone, stuck it on Hawkins's skull, turned it toward Laban Howard and left it there. "But if the skull grinned for that long moment, the black browed 'Captain' glowered back."[286]

When he took the stand in his own defense, Laban Howard's account of what happened that bloody night on Swift Creek sounded as though torn from the pages of *Actual Detective: Stories of Women in Crime*. "I was awakened about an hour later by the sound of a shot. I leaped from bed just as another report sounded. I saw Violet standing over Hawkins with a gun in her hand. I shouted, 'My God, why did you do this?' She replied, 'He had it coming to him for a long time.'" Despite Howard's determination to pin the murder on Violet, the Chesterfield jury had heard enough and returned a verdict of guilty after deliberating only an hour and fifteen minutes. On April 18, 1937, Judge Edwin P. Cox sentenced Howard to life in prison, while Violet and Shelton Howard were set free.[287] While leaving Chesterfield Courthouse, Laban Howard was asked about the trial and maintained his innocence, saying as he was hustled away in handcuffs that the only thing he was guilty of was "being a big sap when I fell for that woman."[288]

It seems Richmond police chief Robert Jordan was among the readers of *Actual Detective: Stories of Women in Crime*, and while paging through the January 1938 issue, he noticed an article by someone he knew quite well. It was Violet Merryman's story of the murder of Ed Hawkins, and among the overheated phrases and melodramatic asides was an account of Violet being taken on a burglary job by her former boyfriend, Laban Howard.[289] The *Times-Dispatch* said that Chief Jordan took exception to Violet's description of sitting in the getaway car and a Richmond cop passing by on the sidewalk, blithely swinging his nightstick and never noticing the robbery taking place. "The story seemed to cast aspersions on the efficiency of the local police," reported the *Times-Dispatch* dryly, "so they brought in the woman and asked her for a more personal account." Obviously alarmed, Violet declared that the article was not accurate and that she was not the author, even signing a notarized statement to that effect. The honor of the Richmond Police Department thereby vindicated, "Then, and only then, was she allowed to leave headquarters."[290]

Chapter 8

VIOLET MERRYMAN

AN OLD WOMAN AND THE DUES SHE PAID

The stifling heat of a Richmond summer is always tough, but the summer of 1942 was especially bad. The temperature got down to 84 degrees on the night of July 19 and soared to 99 the next day. Stores in Richmond sold out of electric fans, and three people died in Norfolk, where the temperature read 101 and stocks of ice disappeared as soon as they were available. Richmonders crowded into movie houses, whose advertisements in the newspapers featured images of snow and icicles to remind the public of their wonderful air conditioning. The Byrd Theater promoted the fact the building was "Carefully Cooled by Carrier," but the slogan of the Ponton Theater was "Where Cool Breezes Blow," apparently signaling that the only relief available in that theater on Hull Street were electric fans.[291] There were probably many empty seats at the Ponton on July 18, 1942, a day where a front-page headline stated flatly, "Last Night Was Hottest in History of Richmond."[292]

The heat was pervasive, and the sun in the cloudless sky above the city offered no relief. It baked the houses and businesses, and hot brick and concrete stayed warm all night before being toasted again the next day. Richmonders panted as they walked along the sidewalks of the city, crossing the street as needed and carefully choosing the route ahead that afforded the most shade. The unrelenting hot weather was hard on people, and Chief of Police E.H. Organ admitted that in the summer of 1942, "Murders, shootings, knifings, burglaries, and other crimes have shown a marked increase in Richmond due to the current heat wave." He explained that the heat makes people "more irritable," and there was a marked rise in the number of assaults among those hot, irritable Richmonders, ranging from simple shoving matches to shootings and stabbings.[293]

As the relentless summer heat degraded the sensibilities of Richmond, those who wanted to escape were attracted to the many bars and dance halls that sprang up just outside the city limits, where surveillance was almost nonexistent and the police were far fewer. Places like the Wigwam, the Spanish Villa, Hillcrest Dance Hall and dozens of nameless beer joints served the thirsty citizens of Richmond and the multitudes of servicemen who came through town that hot summer looking for an ice-cold beer and a good time. That's all that Floyd Green, a local truck driver who lived in the 2500 Block East Franklin Street, wanted when he was waved over to a table at a beer joint by two good-looking women and their friend.

The two coquettish girls Floyd met were Violet Merryman and Violet's friend Emma Dooms. Dooms was a sharp-featured, auburn-haired, freckle-faced girl whose unnerving last name probably came from the family who established Dooms, Virginia. That hamlet is fifteen miles east of Staunton, the city where Emma was born in in 1916.[294] Emma developed a taste for criminality early on, and by age fourteen, she was already an inmate of the Virginia Home and Industrial School for Girls, located just outside Richmond in Bon Air.[295] In 1935, Emma Dooms and a man named J.B. Fisher broke into a corner confectionery store at 21 West Main Street operated by John Djab. They stole money, clothes and Djab's watch and attempted to kill him with a hammer.[296] Arrested and convicted of the crime, Emma was sentenced to the Virginia prison for women in Goochland County for seven years on the charge of felonious assault and five years for burglary. Dooms served six years of her sentence and was released from the women's prison on December 8, 1941.[297]

Green later recalled how, as he drank his beer, Emma Dooms "put the eye on him." He got chummy with Dooms, her friend Violet Merryman with the odd eye and their escort, a "Charles Carter." They said they wanted to go dancing and needed a fourth—would he like to come with them? On the way to the dance, they all got out of the car on a lonesome stretch of Jennie Scher Road in Fulton, and before he could turn around Green was slugged from behind by Carter. He fell into the bushes, and after he woke up, he managed to stagger back out to the road, his hair matted with dried blood. His new friends were long gone. Hastily patting his pockets, he realized that they overlooked his money; holding his throbbing head, Green began to walk unsteadily toward a streetlight in the distance.[298]

Emma Dooms, shown here having a box lunch provided by the Richmond Police Department. *From the* Richmond Times-Dispatch.

"Charles Carter" was actually Harry E. Farris, a twenty-seven-year-old Nebraskan whose life had followed an interesting path before it ended in Richmond, Virginia. Farming apparently held no attraction for Farris, who left Nebraska as a young man. Many of the details of Farris's life in the late 1930s are recorded in the archives of the Abraham Lincoln Brigade, the group of Americans who volunteered to fight on the Republican side in the Spanish Civil War. According to those archives, Farris's occupation was hotel worker and fry cook before he got his passport and sailed to Spain, arriving on July 11, 1937. He volunteered for the Spanish Loyalist Army, where his record says only that he served in various roles such as scout and armorer and notes that at one point he was in Tarraga, in Catalonia. Farris returned to the United States in December 1938, one month after all international volunteers fighting Franco were withdrawn from combat in Spain.[299]

Harry Farris's experience in that especially bitter war, a conflict characterized by reprisals and massacres on both sides, understandably had a profound effect on him. Throughout his meteoric appearance in the public's attention, he appeared indifferent, caring about little more than getting drunk with Emma and Violet, riding around and having a good time. Otherwise, Farris exhibited the benumbed and nihilistic attitude of soldiers of every war who were permanently damaged because they simply saw too much. Today, Farris would have been treated as a victim of post-traumatic stress disorder and received appropriate diagnosis and treatment. No such help was available in the late 1930s for the Americans who fought in Spain, and perhaps because of this, Farris and several people he encountered in Richmond paid a dreadful price.

When Farris returned to the United States, he enlisted in the medical service of the U.S. Army, and a chance assignment brought him to Virginia. Perhaps Farris regarded his enlistment as a continuation

Harry Farris, still in uniform, under arrest and charged with murder. *From the* Richmond Times-Dispatch.

of the same fight against fascism that he saw in Spain. Or maybe the military was just the easiest way to drift for a shell-shocked and indifferent ex-soldier who, after Spain, cared little for society and welcomed the sanctuary of a regulated life. Whatever his motivation to enlist, Farris did not learn much about military discipline during his service in Spain and was AWOL from his temporary base at Byrd Field when he met Violet Merryman. He needed a place to stay, and Violet let him stay with her, embarking on a short, boozy spree in that hot summer of 1942 with horrific consequences. Emma Dooms, their drinking partner, recalled that the first time she met Farris he was in bed with Violet, and in court, Dooms feigned dismay and indignation at the low morals of her companions in crime and debauchery. Despite her shock at such an impropriety, the sight of Violet and Farris in bed together could hardly have been much of a surprise for the worldly and streetwise ex-convict Dooms.[300]

Harry Farris, Emma Dooms and Violet Merryman were a dangerous, sodden mess as they drank their way through the heat wave of July 1942. The only escape was the comparative cool of nightfall, beer, whiskey and boozing their way around Richmond. Their nights were a series of gaudily lit beer joints, roadhouses, motels, barbecue stands, shoddy apartments and always the smell of stale beer, stale smoke, unwashed bodies, cheap perfume

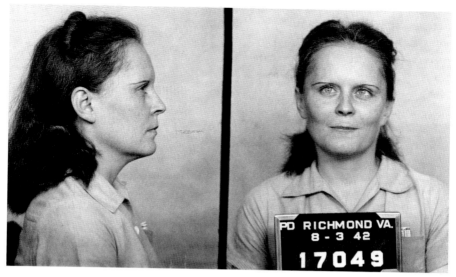

Violet Merryman's mug shot, taken after her arrest in 1942. *From the* Richmond Times-Dispatch.

and ashtrays. Later, as she sat in jail, Emma Dooms made some interestingly frank remarks to reporters that summarized the drunken spree she and her friends went on that summer. When she was asked if they drank so much they didn't know what they were doing, Emma replied, "No, just enough to make us mean and hateful."[301]

William Lamphier found out just how mean and hateful the trio could be. He later said that he was well acquainted with Violet Merryman and had known her for six years before encountering her by chance on Hull Street, so he felt perfectly comfortable in joining her and her friends riding around drinking.[302] Lamphier said he, Violet, Charles Carter and Emma Dooms drove around looking for whiskey, and with Dooms at the wheel, they wound up at a beer joint out on Patterson Avenue. Pulling over and getting out of the car to take a drink, Lamphier was immediately clubbed in the back of the head by Farris, who then rifled his pockets and took about ninety dollars from him as he lay on his face beside the road.[303] Like Floyd Green, with his head pounding and covered with blood, the sweat-soaked Lamphier later managed to drag himself out of the undergrowth to get some help and tell the authorities what happened to him.

Today, the intersection of Wistar Road and West Broad Street looks like thousands of places in the United States with a landscape that features an auto parts store, a strip mall and a car dealership in the distance. The vista is a painfully modern one today, but in 1942, Wistar Road was just another tree-shaded farm lane providing access to Broad Street from the interior of rural Henrico County. Eighty years ago, in the heat of the Virginia summer, it was the scene of a senseless murder. On the morning of July 18, 1942, a Henrico County employee named Tom Collins was walking down Wistar Road when he noticed someone lying face up in the shade, about two hundred yards north of the intersection with Broad Street. It was a man wearing what had been a white summer shirt but which was now soaked with blood. When the Henrico police arrived, they found that the victim had suffered multiple stab wounds that pierced an artery, the heart and the abdomen in several places. The unidentified man died in a flurry of knife blows, but there were no clues and nothing else to do but get the bloodied body out of the heat and send it to Bliley's funeral home.[304]

The day before, Richmonder B.W. Hargrove was hosting a visit from his cousin Frank, a forty-one-year-old Philadelphia Navy Yard mechanic originally from Montpelier in Hanover County. Frank often returned to Virginia to visit his family. His cousin liked to have a good time when he wasn't working, so B.W. thought nothing of it when Frank said that it was too hot to sleep and left the Hargrove house at 2003 Parkwood Avenue about 10:00 p.m. to go out on the town. He didn't come home the following day, and his cousin became increasingly worried, as Frank never stayed out this long when he visited Richmond. Reading the description of a murder victim found beside Wistar Road in Henrico, B.W. Hargrove had a sinking feeling he knew why Frank hadn't returned. He went to Bliley's funeral home and tearfully identified the butchered body under a sheet as that of his cousin.[305] Frank's holiday junket and his life had both ended as quickly and as inexplicably as if he had been hit by lightning, and his brief obituary tersely noted only that he "died suddenly." His Hanover family gathered in the heat at Hopeful Baptist Church two days later to bury him.[306]

The heat wave of the summer of 1942 continued unabated, and Richmonders suffered in what was described as heat that was "breathless" and "sweltering" even during the night. "Many residents sought relief by sleeping in parks throughout the sticky night" reported the *Times-Dispatch*.[307] Violet Merryman, Harry Farris and Emma Dooms rode through the hot night like chain-smoking wraiths, drinking and wandering from beer joint to barbecue stand, from dance hall to nip joint, always looking for the right sucker to approach. They drove what the press later labeled the "death car," a jalopy-like gray 1933 Plymouth with peeling paint and wooden

Frank Hargrove's summer vacation in Richmond ended badly in the hands of Violet Merryman and her murderous drinking companions. *Author's photo.*

spoke wheels that must have looked desperately out of date even by the standards of 1942. The old Plymouth was a Richmond cab owned by John Lozon, who was not a "mean and hateful" drunk like the predatory trio of pals but was smart enough to not ask a lot of questions when his car was borrowed overnight.[308] The two loose and predatory women, combined with the deeply damaged Farris, circulated around the joints looking for victims who were drunk and appeared to have money, like the free-spending, vacationing Frank Hargrove. Much of the information about this alcoholic predation was provided by Emma Dooms, who later testified that they were looking for guys who wouldn't "squawk" if they got robbed and that the money they got from their victims was used for "liquor, gasoline, and a general good time."[309]

About eleven miles from where Frank Hargrove was found, the intersection of Valley Road and Second Street probably looks today very much like it did eighty years ago. The area at the floor of a steep valley is an uneasy mix of aging industrial buildings and stained warehouses, chain link fences and weedy rail lines. Dense woods press in from either side of the street, giving the area even more of a feeling of neglect and dread. Nobody walks through here, and the roadway sparkles in the light from the glass of a thousand broken beer bottles; the trees are low, and the sidewalk is rank with weeds in long stretches from decades of disuse. Hours before the hot dawn of July 19, 1942, the police received a report of someone screaming here on the hillside at the far northern end of Richmond's Second Street.

Vinicio Bichi was a thirty-six-year-old clerk in a confectionery located beside the Colonial Theater on Broad Street. He was born in a tiny village in Tuscany in 1906 and immigrated with his family to Richmond in 1921.[310] In 1940, he was living with his mother on North Eleventh Street, but by his last summer in 1942, Bichi was finally able to afford a room of his own in a house at 3412 Delaware Avenue. His draft card stated that Bichi weighed 125 pounds and was five feet, five inches tall. Standing at the corner of Eighth and Broad today, you can imagine the slim man with dark hair and dark eyes inside the plate glass, gazing out at the people and the traffic and the streetcars and wondering if selling Coca-Colas and cigarettes on the side of Broad Street was all that life would ever offer.[311]

That night, though, Vincio Bichi was enjoying himself, having had a few drinks, and later was seen smiling as he climbed into an oddly rough-looking car at First and Cary Streets. He was probably delighted to meet new friends, to be chatting with attractive women and to be invited for a ride to somewhere they could get a drink, talk and maybe dance. He may have imagined that his astonishing good luck in stumbling into the girl who had an odd cast to one eye but who was so very friendly. The whole group were all very jolly, and they immediately agreed to get some whiskey and go for a ride.

A man named Alonzo Brown lived not far through the woods from the intersection of Second Street and Valley Roads. Somewhere out in the fireflies, crickets and the hot, dark night, someone was shouting, "They're killing me!" Brown rushed down the street to see what was going on and encountered a man, apparently wearing a scarlet shirt, facedown beside the road near an old car. A woman wearing a pink pajama outfit was standing over him and told Brown that her friend was drunk. There was also a disheveled and wild-eyed man standing in the road who told Brown in no uncertain terms to get out of there or he was going to be killed. Just before he turned to run, Brown glanced down and realized that the man on the ground dressed in red was actually wearing a blood-soaked white shirt.[312]

The last glimpse of Vincio Bichi is as a murder victim, grotesquely sprawled beside the road at Second and Valley, almost but not quite beheaded by having his throat deeply cut from ear to ear, with a terrible fan of blood sweeping down his shirt. There was blood everywhere: blood on the sidewalk, sprinkling the leaves and all over his clothes. Testifying in court, Dooms said that Violet and Harry went with Bichi into the woods armed with a hammer and a kitchen knife and came back covered in blood. They got blood on the car and blood on Dooms, and all three went back to Dooms's apartment in the 900 block of West Broad Street, took off all their clothes and scrubbed themselves. Then they cleaned the blood out of Lozon's car.[313]

The hot nightmare that was this weekend of bloodstained barhopping must have struck a chord with Violet. Standing with a hammer in her

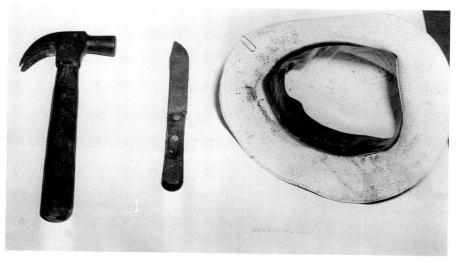

A display of evidence: the two murder weapons used to kill Vincio Bichi and the victim's crushed and bloody hat. *From the* Richmond Times-Dispatch.

hand as Farris went to work on the screaming Bichi, Violet must have been reminded of another bad, hot summer night when Laban Howard stalked determinedly across the room in that cabin in Chesterfield to get Ed Hawkins to shut up. She had now seen three men killed in front of her, and even with all the lost weekends and blackout drinking, she could not erase the picture of Hawkins pleading for his life, the stab wounds Farris unleashed on Frank Hargrove and that spreading bib of red on his shirt as Harry grunted with effort and pulled back on the blade under Bichi's chin. To the smell of sweat and flat beer and spilled whiskey was added that awful and too-familiar metallic tang of spilled blood in the air.

The police began a search for two women accompanied by a man who were reportedly seen in Bichi's company. Detective Sergeant Garton of Richmond said that they had a good description of the three, and in Henrico County, Chief W.J. Hedrick was quoted as saying he felt the murder of Hargrove and Bichi may be related since the victims were found in similar circumstances, although miles apart.[314] The technical description of a horrific wound that almost took his head off stated that Bichi's cause of death was "hemorrhage due to stab wound of neck." His death certificate also noted the final disposition of the hapless immigrant who looked for companionship and found only violent death: burial at Richmond's Mount Calvary Catholic Cemetery on July 21, 1942.[315]

Two days later, the police received a tip from an anonymous source that led them to Harry Farris. His name came up when the police consulted the Military Police Detachment, which kept order among the many service men and women who came through the Richmond area. An inquiry about a "Corporal Carter" who was absent without leave did not produce any records with the MPs, but the description closely resembled that of another serviceman who was missing: Corporal Harry Farris. The Military Police picked Farris up and turned him over to the Richmond authorities, where he was questioned by Detective Captain Garton. Farris soon confessed to killing Hargrove and Bichi and implicated Emma Dooms and Violet Merryman as his accomplices. Farris's complete candor and indifference regarding a possible defense in the face of two murder charges is breathtaking, and he apparently felt no compunction to defer to a lawyer. "Farris told me," Garton said, "that he learned to cut and stab in vital spots while fighting with the Loyalist Army in Spain and added to this knowledge by service with a Medical Corps detachment of the United States Army."[316]

Violet was arrested in Columbia, South Carolina, on August 2, 1942, where she had been held in jail for several days, charged with public

Vincio Bichi's grave in his family's plot at Richmond's Mount Calvary Catholic Cemetery.
Author's photo.

drunkenness after having fled Richmond with Emma Dooms in John Lozon's cab. She was once again betrayed by that distinctive cast to one eye, making her instantly identifiable to the authorities. The ancient cab was found sixty miles away and contained evidence, including the clothes Violet and Emma were described as wearing during their murderous weekend.[317]

Captain Garton interviewed Violet upon her return to Richmond and told the press that she was "sick, dejected, and thoroughly tired out."[318] To Violet, it all must have seemed like an insane run, another bloody, drunken, stupid spree that she was mixed up in, but perhaps she also knew that this time all the beer and whiskey in Richmond couldn't ward off the consequences. Violet's drinking and involvement with Laban Howard was nothing more than the beginning of a long, beery and bloody descent from factory girl to accessory to murder, with more than a few arrests along the way. Meeting Harry Farris and Emma Dooms proved the perfect accelerant for the inexorable downhill slide toward darkness, murder, prison and perhaps the electric chair.

The newspapers had a field day with Violet and dredged up her role years before in the conviction of Laban Howard for the grisly murder of Ed Hawkins. Violet once again was referred to with disdain as "the Merryman woman" in the press. A Richmond newspaper ran a photo of a claw hammer, a large kitchen knife and the flattened and blood-spattered hat that Bichi was wearing when he was invited into the Plymouth with Violet; the caption identified it as the hammer Violet was "allegedly prepared to use if Harry Farris failed to kill Vincio Bichi."[319] A list of "October Highlights" of future events in Richmond for the month included a statement by Lieutenant G.W. Mast warning that "an army of prostitutes have invaded Virginia and cost the Navy 18,000 lost man days," predicted a run on state liquor stores before the imposition of a federal tax and reminded readers of the upcoming court appearance of Violet Merryman, calling her "the accused 'hammer woman'" in the Bichi trial.[320] Violet even made the national news, where in New York the *Daily News* headline read "Girl Who Attracts Murderers Is Mixed Up in More Killings," saying that the "Red-headed Violet Merryman, the woman who likes murderers—or perhaps it's just murders—faces trial here shortly."[321]

The Richmond police arrested Emma Dooms on July 31 as she attempted to return to her apartment in the 900 block of West Broad Street. When told she had been indicted by a grand jury along with Violet and Farris for the death of Vincio Bichi, Dooms had a moment of grim candor, predicting, "I deserve just what I'll get." When asked what kind of sentence she might receive for her part in the murder of the harmless confectionery clerk, the unflinching Dooms guessed "maybe 35 years," never imagining that she would not see freedom again and would die decades later in an insane asylum. At the time, though, the canny Dooms was able to calculate her odds and resolved to cooperate with the authorities as the only way to moderate her punishment. "I want the public to know," the hard-looking redhead told the press, "that I am willing to aid the police any way I can, now or later." When asked what she meant about the "later" remark, Dooms said evasively, "They might find something else," meaning the police might want to hang her and her drunken, murderous companions with the death of Frank Hargrove in addition to the Bichi killing.[322]

All three of the murderers were now held in various area jails. Farris, in contrast to his crimes, described by Captain Garton as "savage," sat impassively in his cell, eating well, sleeping well and not asking for any special privileges. Garton dismissed the idea of Farris as an honorably shell-shocked soldier and saw him in a different, more pragmatic way: "Farris was mixed up with women and brawled with them. He was after women, whiskey, beer—and money."[323] Farris's trial for the murder of Vincio Bichi began

Emma Dooms leads police to a storm drain on the corner of Lombardy Street and Floyd Avenue, where they recovered the knife used to cut Vinico Bichi's throat. *From the* Richmond Times-Dispatch.

on September 17, 1942, in the Richmond Hustings Court on the second floor of the building now known as Old City Hall. The star witness against Farris was Emma Dooms, who testified for more than an hour about the scheme to rob the drunken men whom Farris, Violet and Emma collected from Richmond bars and beer joints. She said that Violet always played the role of bait, Dooms stayed in the car when Violet and Farris got out of the car with victims like Vincio Bichi and she watched as the pair strode on off into the dark behind their victim, carrying a knife and a hammer.[324]

Witnesses described being attacked by the trio under very similar circumstances, and others testified as to Bichi's wounds. A surprise witness said that they saw Bichi happily getting into a car with a woman in a pink pajama outfit. In cross-examination, Emma Dooms was asked if perhaps she was the woman in the pink outfit who had been seen standing over the nearly decapitated Bichi, making her furious with the prosecutor. "I don't wear pink pajamas!" she snapped, "I'm a red headed woman and I wear brown and yellow!"[325] Throughout the trial, Farris, neatly dressed in uniform, watched Emma Dooms and the rest of the proceedings without demonstrating much interest aside from an ironic sense of humor. When the jury went out at 4:45 p.m., he joked with bystanders about how fickle juries could be, but the reporter observing Farris noticed that he declined to guess what was coming. However, Farris knew exactly what was coming. The jury was back in an hour, and Harry Farris was condemned to death for the Bichi murder.[326] "I don't think I done it." Farris said as he was led from the courtroom, "I have a clear conscience. Of course, I was drunk and might have done it, but I don't think I did. If this is the way I got to go out, I guess that's all there is to it. It don't matter much."[327]

Emma Dooms was also the principal witness in the trial of Violet Merryman for Bichi's death, and the proceedings began on the morning of October 26, 1942. The testimony was much the same, with Dooms recounting the drunken spree with Harry and Violet. Dooms's testimony became more sensational during Violet's trial, and she added lurid details, such as Violet urging Farris to cut some loose ends and kill Emma in her bathroom where the three of them were working on scrubbing Vincio Bichi's

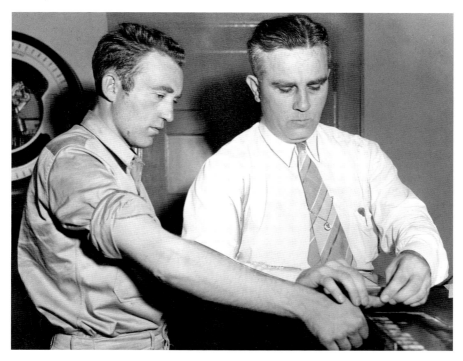

Harry Farris is fingerprinted at Richmond police headquarters. *From the* Richmond Times-Dispatch.

blood out of their clothing. She described Violet as "drinking all the time; she had an insane temper; a mean temper."[328]

Unlike Harry, Violet took the stand in her defense. "Costumed almost entirely in black, her brunette hair freshened by a permanent wave, she attempted to excuse her role in the Bichi killing, the slaying of Frank Hargrove, and offered the one defense she could think that might save her from the electric chair: she was drunk the whole time." Violet denied that she was out trolling the bars for prey: "We were just out driving around, drinking, and having a good time." The prosecutor, incredulous, asked her, "Is that the only explanation you can give the jury?" It seemed to be the best thing that either Violet or her lawyer could come up with, and she repeatedly told the court, "We had been drinking, constantly drinking." Describing her version of Bichi's death, Violet said, "I was rather tight…I took four drinks at the scene of the murder, I was staggering."[329]

In his closing remarks, Gray Haddon, the Commonwealth's attorney, called for the death penalty for Violet Merryman. "They planned to get easy money by enticing men with what appeals to men," he thundered. "If ever it was intended that the extreme penalty be given, the evidence in this case seems to justify it." The jury came back with a verdict of guilty, but instead of the death sentence the prosecutor demanded, Violet Merryman was sentenced to twenty-five years in the state penitentiary.[330]

Later that week, the whole process was repeated in a Henrico County courtroom as Violet Merryman was put on trial for her role in the murder of Frank Hargrove. More lurid details went on the record, as Emma Dooms helped bury her former drinking pal with additional years' confinement, with her testimony starting to sound theatrically hardboiled. Emma said when she glanced down the shoulder of Wistar Road, she saw Farris's sunburnt arm coming across Hargrove's white shirt, then Hargrove groaned and fell on the ground. "If you look, I'll give you the same," snarled Violet Merryman in Emma's testimony. "'I won't look,' I said, and Violet said, 'you better not.'" Violet took the stand and again relied on her intoxication as her best defense. "The husky-voiced brunette again insisted she was completely innocent, saying she had only been out 'riding with Harry' and that it was Dooms who helped Farris roll Hargrove's body into the ditch beside Wistar Road." The jury was unimpressed, the verdict was guilty and the sentence for Violet Merryman was thirty years.[331]

In April 1943, Emma Dooms went on trial in Henrico County for the death of Frank Hargrove, and she chose to forego a jury trial when she appeared before Judge Julian Gunn. Perhaps she read in the *New York Daily*

News that "[n]o trial date has been set for Miss Dooms, who proved helpful to the prosecution at every opportunity. It was assumed that, should she be tried, her sentence would be comparable to that given a shop-lifter."[332] In contrast, Commonwealth's Attorney H.M. Radcliff said that if she pleaded guilty, he would simply produce all the evidence of her guilt, including her own admissions as to her role in Hargrove's death. If she attempted to plead innocent, Radcliff said he would ask for the death penalty.[333]

On April 8, 1942, the day of her hearing in Henrico, Dooms's lawyer, Percy Smith, made a last-minute attempt to have his client's charges reduced to being an accessory to murder, but that was rejected by Judge Gunn. When finally asked how she pleaded to the charge of murder, Dooms responded in a low voice and said, "Guilty." Dooms's attempt to buy leniency by testifying against Violet and Harry and then throwing herself on the mercy of the court failed spectacularly, much to her dismay. "The befreckled, auburn-haired woman appeared visibly surprised" when she received the same thirty-year sentence as Violet for Hargrove's death.[334]

By October 1943, Harry Farris had lost the last of seven appeals of his case made by his court-appointed attorney L. Gleason Gianniny, who had taken Farris's cause without success to the Virginia Supreme Court and then the U.S. Supreme Court. When Governor Colgate Dardin refused to intervene, Farris's fate was sealed, and his execution was scheduled for October 15.[335] Later, Farris's lawyer revealed some previously unknown facts about the condemned man, such as he had a daughter who was being raised by Farris's former wife and her new husband, who was a friend of Farris and a fellow volunteer in the war in Spain. Gianniny said that although he had long and extensive talks with Harry, "I have never been able to fathom Farris' innermost being. I believe him when he said he did not remember the week of crime when Bichi was killed. However, he was the strangest man I have ever known." In all those hours of talk between the condemned man and his lawyer, he only mentioned Violet Merryman and Emma Dooms once, ruefully saying, "I wish I had never met them."[336]

Harry Farris was executed in Virginia's electric chair on October 15, 1943. He told his lawyer that he would go to the chair calmly when the time came, and Gianniny believed him, saying, "The man has no nerves." No details of Farris's last moments were released to the public other than a brief statement from penitentiary superintendent Major W. Frank Smyth: "Farris was pronounced dead at 8:40 o'clock this morning." Gianniny, the state penitentiary prison chaplain and some of Gianniny's friends took up a collection and paid for his plot and burial at Richmond's Forest Lawn

Harry Farris's grave marker at Richmond's Forest Lawn Cemetery, with the epitaph "He Was a Soldier of Democracy." *Author's collection.*

Cemetery. The epitaph on Farris's grave marker reads, "He Was a Soldier of Democracy," reflecting what Farris must have regarded as his most noble days, fighting fascism in Spain.

The trial of Emma Dooms for the death of Vincio Bichi began five days after Farris's execution. She again pleaded guilty to the Bichi murder and threw herself on the mercy of the court, and for this crime Dooms received another twenty years in jail, to run concurrently with the thirty she got for her part in killing Frank Hargrove. This contrasted with the total of fifty-five years that Violet Merryman was sentenced to serve for the same crimes, showing how the tough little girl with freckles and formidable last name had indeed made the better deal when she informed on her fellow defendants.[337]

Emma Dooms once recalled that she met Violet Merryman "in Goochland, where all rats are found,"[338] meaning the prison west of Richmond then known as the Virginia State Industrial Farm for Women. Both Dooms and Merryman were inmates here for years, and we don't know what measures were taken to keep them apart since it was largely through Dooms's testimony that Violet spent most of her life in Goochland County. Although not far from their old boozy haunts, the prison must have seemed as though it was on a different planet from the beer joints and dance halls they once knew so well. The facility emphasized work and education with an element of religious practice, and there were few idle hours. Women could learn housekeeping or culinary skills or gain practical nursing experience in the clinic. Classes were held from reading and writing basics to high school level.[339] The seasons crept over the rolling Goochland landscape, relentlessly turning them first brown and green, coming and going with winter's chill and summer's heat, but there was never a cold beer in sight for the two former carousers, barflies and killers.

By late 1962, Emma Dooms, age forty-six, was evidently in declining mental health when she was transferred from the woman's prison in Goochland to Southwestern State Hospital.[340] Originally known as Southwestern Lunatic Asylum, the facility was in Marion, Virginia. There, Emma and her fate disappear behind the high walls of Virginia's privacy laws, but there is no evidence that she was released; Dooms probably died in the Marion mental hospital. Her record at the Social Security Administration shows that Dooms made an application for benefits in 1976 and notes the date of her death at age seventy-three in 1989 but gives no information as to her location or circumstances.[341]

Violet Merryman applied for and received parole on two occasions during her years of imprisonment, two opportunities that she squandered either because of her bad attitude or a simple inability to deal with the world on "the outside." Her casual attitude and glib explanations of what went wrong during these glimpses of liberty probably ensured her return to prison. She told a reporter that she had been on parole for about a year in 1960 and working in Culpepper when she was simply "caught" on a bus to Lynchburg, in violation of the terms of her parole. She was given a second chance five years later and was working in Charlottesville when she got in a "fuss" with her landlady—an incident serious enough to get her returned once more to prison.[342] Even as a young woman, in and out of jail, Violet was drawn to losers and criminals and the seamier side of life, but after decades of hardening behind bars, she seemed completely unsuitable for life in the world beyond the confines of what became her home in Goochland County.

In 1967, Violet Merryman finally completed her sentence for the death of Vincio Bichi, now in his grave for twenty-five years, and the sixty-year-old former brunette's hair was snow white as she began her term for her role in the murder of Frank Hargrove. A newspaper noted at the time that Violet was "believed to be the longest imprisoned woman in Virginia history."[343] The story of the prisoner once disdainfully referred to as "the Merryman woman" was reexamined in the papers once again, going back to her role in the murder of Ed Hawkins thirty years before.[344]

Violet engaged an attorney named William C. Carter, who filed a writ in 1969 to have her released. Carter cited publicity in Richmond newspapers surrounding Violet's trial for the Bichi murder and alleged incompetence by the two lawyers who represented her during her trial for the death of Hargrove.[345] Violet and her attorney claimed that the jury in the Hargrove trial ("all old men," sniffed Violet, disdainfully) were influenced by the sensational coverage of the Bichi trial only two days before. She said that she never met her lawyers before the day of her trial, and Violet's memory was that she was called to court in morning and was "back in jail by lunchtime."[346] When asked by the Commonwealth's attorney why she waited almost twenty-eight years to file a petition for her release, and just for a second, her response is one of the few times her unfiltered, true voice is heard. "My people got angry with me when I got in all this trouble," Violet explained, and refused to give her any money to hire a lawyer. She said she now depended on Social Security to fund her appeal.[347]

In April 1970, Violet's filings for release were denied. No longer "the Merryman woman," Violet became "Mrs. Merryman" in her newspaper coverage during this period. The now grandmotherly looking Violet was brought from her prison in Goochland back to court in the old Henrico Courthouse on Main Street where she had been convicted so many years before. Despite her matronly appearance, Violet was still regarded as a dangerous criminal by the unsympathetic judge E. Ballard Baker, who said, "Mrs. Merryman's testimony on this point [is] unbelievable but is also contradicted by some of the very newspaper articles she files to support her claims. Certainly, no court has to accept the word of Mrs. Merryman, whose testimony with respect to other matters is demonstrably false and who waits for a quarter of a century to complain."[348] Her appeals thoroughly dismissed, Violet Merryman was helped into the back seat of a Henrico police car, and the aging reminder of a different, more desperate era in Richmond was again returned to prison.

The year 1972 found Violet not only finally out of prison but also a wife. Perhaps she was paroled in the wake of the publicity that named her the oldest female convict in Virginia or for health reasons, but in May of that year, she married George Thomas Eades, a sixty-two-year-old bachelor and retired window salesman from Lynchburg. How George Eades and Violet met and agreed to marry is not known, but after the ceremony at a Baptist church in Petersburg, the couple returned to live in George's bungalow in

Lynchburg. George Eades and Violet were married fifteen years before his death in August 1987.[349]

Violet Merryman Eades died on September 3, 1988, in a Lynchburg nursing home at age eighty-two. Her occupation is listed on her death certificate as "housewife," and in the block on the form that asks for "kind of business or industry," it just says simply, "home."[350] The bland domesticity of this response makes it seem possible that Violet may have finally found some measure of comfort and quiet at the end of a long life that had offered little of either. Violet and her husband, George, are buried together in unmarked graves at Lynchburg's Presbyterian Cemetery.

Chapter 9

THE CRASH OF IMPERIAL AIRLINES FLIGHT 201/8

DEATH IN THE HENRICO PINES

Had they lived, by now they would all be in their eighties, enjoying retirement, doting on grandchildren and probably looking back at typically American lives from the vantage point of old age. A few may have remained in the military and continued to serve their country, a career that would have begun for them in November 1961. For many on the trip to South Carolina, this was their first plane ride, but had they lived, by now the passage of sixty years would have gently buffed away the memory of how they got to basic training, and even the novelty of Imperial Airlines flight 201/8 would after all those years seemed as forgettable as a routine bus ride.

Instead, they all died in the middle of the night, in the piney woods east of Richmond, unable to move and trapped in a burning metal tube. Instead of living to a ripe old age, seventy-four young men died on November 8, 1961, burning to death or dying from smoke inhalation. It was one of this country's worst air disasters, and it occurred in the woods of Henrico County just a few miles from what is now Richmond International Airport. Today, dense pines have again shrouded the site where so many died, but the memorial that recalls the young men in that burning plane is miles away, in downtown Richmond.

In the years after World War II, the United States was overstocked with cheap surplus airplanes and awash in experienced but unemployed former military pilots who decided to go into the aviation business. "It looked like a sure thing, said the *New York Daily News*, "a couple of pilots could get together, buy a surplus DC-3 for $15,000—and they were in business."[351]

These became known as "nonskeds." This informal term for non-scheduled flights was used for airlines that operated without set schedules but instead flew on demand in various degrees of airworthiness.

A favorite plane of the nonskeds was the Lockheed Constellation, a World War II design with a distinctive triple tail. The "Connie" had originally been designed for a long-range troop transport and was cheaply converted to a civilian airliner. The last Constellation was produced in 1958 and was going out of service with the major carriers, but for the nonsked airlines, with their mercenary practices and cost-cutting maintenance, anything that would cheaply carry a lot of passengers was ideal. In 1951, a surplus Constellation developed engine trouble over eastern Virginia. The Eastern Airlines pilots made a successful belly landing without injuries in a muddy field at Curles Neck Farm, fifteen miles south of the Richmond airport.[352]

On the morning of Wednesday, November 8, 1961, the Civil Aeronautics Board (CAB) opened hearings in Washington into the nonsked airline industry, focusing on Imperial Airlines. The members of the board stated that they would be looking into the business practices of the little airline, its financial condition and, above all, the safety and maintenance aspects of Imperial.[353] The same day began early for twenty-eight young men in Paterson, New Jersey. They assembled at the city hall to begin the induction process for entering the U.S. Army. Their photograph was taken as they waited; captured in that moment, their faces reflect a variety of expressions as they sit or stand against a wall. Most smile broadly for the camera, while a few appear reflective. One or two have overnight bags, and some smoke cigarettes, indictive of their nascent adulthood. Most wear the white socks and loafers so typical of the day. This could be a photograph of a fraternity or a high school team anywhere in the country. At 8:00 a.m., the group arrived by bus at the army processing center in Newark, but six were sent home because of an outstanding parking ticket, an undisclosed medical condition or some incomplete paperwork.[354]

After a long day of waiting around, the young men boarded Imperial Airlines Flight 201/8.[355] At 6:22 p.m., it took off from Newark. The Wilkes-Barre/Scranton airport was the next stop and then on to Baltimore, where seventeen more recruits boarded the plane, which turned south, back to where the flight originated in Columbia, South Carolina.[356] On board the Imperial Airlines plane were five crew members: Captain Ronald Conway, Captain James Greenlee, Flight Engineer William Poythress, a student flight engineer named Peter Clark and flight attendant Linda Johns. Conway, age twenty-nine, served as a private in the air force and afterward flew "for various small

Of these twenty-eight young men who assembled at Paterson, New Jersey, twenty-two of them would be dead within hours in the crash of Imperial Airlines flight 201/8. *Author's collection.*

airlines." In 1956, he married a Regina Airlines flight attendant; like their other crew members, they made their home in Miami.[357] James Greenlee was the oldest in the crew at age forty-five, a World War II veteran who had risen to rank of major in the air force. Thirty-year-old flight engineer Poythress, like Conway, was a Korean War–era air force veteran.[358]

The presence of two pilots with the rank of captain on Imperial 201/8 was unusual. Usually having two senior pilots would be thought an advantage, but conflicting statements and conflicting decisions would be cited as one of the reasons for chaos in the cockpit later in the flight. As one finding put it, the unusual mix of crewmembers led to the "lack of command coordination and decision."[359] Contributing to this confusion was the presence of Clark, the flight engineer trainee, who performed various tasks at the orders of Poythress and Greenlee without the knowledge of Conway, who was ostensibly in command of the plane.[360]

As Imperial 201/8 traveled down the East Coast toward South Carolina, a cascading series of problems began, beginning with an alarm that power was being lost to one of the plane's four engines. What followed was termed "a tragedy of errors" that began with fuel starvation, and Poythress ordered

Clark, his trainee, to go to the passenger section of the plane and open the cross-feed valve that would have enabled all four engines to draw on any fuel tank. Clark came back to the cockpit and said that he would have to have a screwdriver to access the valve. Critically, Greenlee stopped him, saying, "Don't open that valve. You have good pressure on 1 and 2; leave it there." Conway later said that he did not hear the exchange between Poythress and Clark and never knew that the valve stayed closed.[361] Later, in testimony, Conway was asked if the cross-feed valve *had* been opened, did he think power would have been restored to two of the plane's engines. "I would have much rather seen that valve open," Conway blandly replied, a masterpiece of understatement considering what was soon to follow.[362]

The confusion in the cockpit continued, and Conway prepared to land at Byrd Airport in Richmond. Contacting the control tower at Byrd, Conway was told to use the longest runway, but abruptly and without Conway knowing it, Greenlee chose to use a different, shorter runway to land, and the plane turned and banked to get lined up properly. Despite their difficulties in the cockpit, the flight crew expected to land safely. Flight attendant Linda Johns was not told to give emergency evacuation instructions to the passengers, as they were still on two engines and capable of a landing on the runway. The crew next attempted to put the landing gear down, but this did not respond; unfortunately, they did not know that the plane was equipped with a special control for lowering the wheels in just such an emergency.[363]

By then, it was becoming too late. For those who noticed, the sight of trainee Clark kneeling in the aisle and unsuccessfully trying to gain access to the cross-feed valve must have done nothing for the passengers' confidence in this airplane or its crew. The change in pitch of the four propeller engines also must have been quite noticeable inside the plane, let alone the ominous silence from one side of the fuselage after two engines quit completely. As the pilots fought the controls for a second pass at the runway, the lights of Byrd Airport would have flashed by at a crazy angle while the plane executed a wide, banking turn and then banked again sharply to the right, out over the utter blackness of the pines. Just before the impact, the third of four engines stopped. There must have been just the slightest pause of terrifying quiet, followed by a scream from the one remaining engine as it desperately accelerated, forcing the nose of the plane up. Flight 201/8 managed to claw its way up to seven hundred feet above Henrico County. And then it fell into the woods below at a speed of just over one hundred miles per hour.

Conway called out to Greenlee, "I see the trees coming," before the plane started clipping treetops. "The impact didn't feel too severe to me….I hit the control wheel, but I immediately came back to a seated position and the first thing I thought of was the impact didn't seem like hardly anything. But the immediately I realized the airplane was on fire. Everything caught fire immediately. It was bright as daylight outside."[364]

Conway jerked open the cockpit door into the airplane cabin, but it was a mass of flame and smoke inside. Turning to the exterior crew door of the cockpit, they threw it open to a vista of flames as far as they could see. Conway, a small man, opened the sliding cockpit window and managed to get through it and fall on the ground outside the plane. Squeezing through the tiny window to safety wasn't an option for Greenlee and Poythress, who leaped out of the crew door into the flaming woods outside. Trainee Clark and Johns, the flight attendant, were inside the burning cabin with the panicked passengers.[365]

Minutes before, A.P. Webb, who was a customer service representative for another airline, stepped outside his office at Byrd Airport and watched the stricken Constellation settle lower and lower and then disappear beyond the trees in the distance beyond the edge of the airport. "Suddenly the horizon lit up. After the pinkish glow died, a great ball of flames came up."[366] John Wilson, a former Richmond fireman, served on the Byrd Airport emergency crew and was alerted that a plane in distress was expected at the airport. "It went straight down," Wilson recalled, "and disappeared in a ball of flame.…It must have gone 300 feet in the air." Wilson and his team rushed for the crash truck and got as close to the burning, exploding airplane as they could, guided by what looked like an enormous bonfire in the distance. Then they continued into the dense woods on foot. They found Conway and Poythress, both burned and coughing, wandering in the flickering light and wild shadows of the trees, about forty yards from the wreckage. One fireman recalled, "The heat and flames were terrible. They drove us back. There wasn't anything we could do for those inside."[367] The *Richmond News Leader* reporter on the scene concluded glumly, "It made no real difference when the firemen got there. Theirs was primarily a job of fire containment."

Hampering the firefighting efforts were hundreds of onlookers and rubberneckers who converged on the scene, wandering the woods and whose cars choked nearby roads. "The scene was a macabre one—with policemen by the score, firemen by the dozens, the curious by the hundreds, gathered about the wreckage, the generators, the spotlights, the fire apparatus. They had come through brush, mud, water, and gullies for half a mile. The curious came from all possible directions through the woods, defying police and their snarling dogs."[368] The newspaper noted that the fire burned for four more

Police and soldiers secure the scene of the wreck of Imperial Airlines 201/8. One of the few recognizable features in the wreckage is the distinctive twin tail section of the Lockheed Constellation airplane. *Author's collection.*

hours and it was 9:30 a.m. the next morning before the first body could be removed from the wreckage. "Four soldiers carried the plastic-covered recruit soldier through 200 yards of underbrush. By mid-afternoon half the bodies had been removed from the wreckage. All were totally burned."[369]

The news of the crash of Imperial 2101/8 hit rural Pennsylvania like a hammer blow. Irving Langel was the chief clerk at the Wilkes-Barre induction center for young men going in the army and recalled November 8 with utter disbelief. "I spent the whole day with these boys, interviewing them, issuing them their service numbers, seeing them fingerprinted and signing their records. I took them to lunch and dinner." Langel was having a cup of coffee in a diner in a Pennsylvania town called Suburban Plains when a bulletin came on the television in the corner. "I ran up to the set to hear more. And I almost collapsed because a couple of hours earlier I had been with them, shaking hands and saying goodbye."[370]

The toll was dreadful in little towns in Pennsylvania, New Jersey and Maryland where "all night shocked, tearful, pleading relatives of the recruits placed pathetic telephone calls to newspaper, wire service and radio station offices as well as aviation officials in Washington and Richmond and the airline's small headquarters in Miami. 'Are they dead or are they alive?' many of the voices pleaded. 'What happened?'"[371] Back in Passaic, New Jersey, the headline of the local paper screamed in huge type "Flaming Plane Crash Kills 22 Local Army Recruits" and listed the grim statistics from the area:

fourteen dead from Passaic, five from nearby Clifton and one each from the nearby towns of Rutherford, Garfield and Wayne. A small map in the Passaic *Herald News* helpfully located Richmond so the readers of could see where Imperial Airlines flight 201/8 ended in the Henrico woods.[372]

The morning of November 9 saw news of the crash continue to spread, with a variety of horrified reactions ranging from "stunned and stony silence, with screams, with hysteria, with dull red anger." One enraged parent screamed at a reporter, "I don't want any publicity. I want my son back. Give the generals the publicity. They murdered him in one day, those lousy -------!"[373] Another parent recalled how their son commented that the group waiting for transport that morning looked like a Passaic High School reunion. "Then he got on the bus and that was the last his parents saw of him."[374] The fingerprints of the recruits, taken only the day before, were quietly collected by an agent of the FBI and sent to Richmond to aid in the grim task of trying to identify the charred bodies of the children of places like Bethlehem and Nazareth, Baltimore and Brooklyn, Washington, D.C., Windgap and Jersey City.[375]

The Lehigh Valley area of Pennsylvania was hit especially hard, and the statistics hinted at the enormity of the loss. Twenty-seven families in the area lost a son, and one family lost two sons. "Forty-four men and boys lost a brother and two others lost two brothers. Thirty-four women and girls lost a brother, and one other lost two brothers."[376] The little towns of the Lehigh Valley braced for a bleak holiday season with so many missing faces around the Thanksgiving table. That holiday week, another group of inductees was assembled in Newark. This time, however, they were going by bus to meet a train that would take them to South Carolina. They posed for a group photo on the risers where so many now dead young men had stood just a few weeks before. This time, almost none of the young men are smiling for the photographer.[377]

Back in Richmond, a road had been built through the woods to retrieve the wreckage of the airplane. A bulldozer and several large flatbed trucks hauled the debris to the United Airlines hangar at Byrd Airport for examination by the Civil Aeronautics Board experts.[378] The grim, painstaking task of identifying the burned bodies of the victims was immediately begun by acting Virginia chief medical examiner Dr. H.H. Karnitschnig and his staff at the Medical College Hospital. Families of the victims were asked to provide an inventory of personal effects, and what horror they must have felt welling up inside them as they gathered their lists of the little talismans that might identify their dead sons and brothers:

"A wallet, a watch, a letter, a cigarette lighter, a cross, a bracelet."[379] The corpse of the only woman on board Imperial 201/8, the nineteen-year-old flight attendant Linda Johns, was among the first identified and returned to her hometown of Inverness, Florida.[380]

When released by the medical examiner, the bodies of the young soldiers were taken to the army base at Fort Lee, south of Richmond, and flag-draped caskets began to arrive literally by the truckload.[381] "Army officers saluted, and enlisted men snapped their rifles to present arms when the procession rolled by." As the caskets were placed in the base field house, an armed guard was stationed around the building, and military identification experts and civilian morticians went to work. One employee of a store near the army base entrance slumped against a doorframe and watched the grim parade of trucks enter the gates. "I don't want to read, see or hear any more about this," she said, "It's all so terrible."[382]

The tragic story of the crash of the Imperial Airlines plane was only made worse with the release of the medical examiner's findings. None of the dead was killed by the impact of the airplane in the pine trees. Even though "many bodies were piled in a jumble in the rear of the plane," autopsies revealed very few broken bones among the dead. Horrifically, all the victims suffocated due to carbon monoxide poisoning, and then their

Fort Lee, Virginia. An honor guard stands beside the first of dozens of flag-draped caskets containing the victims of Flight 201/8. *From the* Richmond Times-Dispatch.

bodies burned.[383] The terse wording typed on the death certificate for Peter Clark, the flight engineer trainee, tells the whole story of Imperial Airlines flight 201/8: "DESCRIBE HOW DEATH OCCURRED—airplane crash. PLACE OF INJURY—deep woods. CAUSE OF DEATH—carbon monoxide poisoning."[384]

The Civil Aeronautics Board moved with unprecedented swiftness to determine the cause of the crash of the Imperial Airlines flight. It met, dramatically, on top what was then one of the tallest buildings in Richmond: the roof garden on the sixteenth floor of the Hotel John Marshall. At Byrd Airport, investigators and technicians continued to pore over the charred remains of the Lockheed Constellation and submit their findings on the physical evidence, the record of the plane itself, its crew, the weather, all radio traffic and eye witnesses.[385] While the Civil Aeronautics Board investigation continued, in Washington, U.S. Secretary of Defense Robert S. McNamara issued tighter controls and oversight of the military's use of contracted, unscheduled airlines, forcing them to come up to the safety standards of commercial airlines.[386]

Even before the release of the CAB investigation into the accident, TIME magazine ran a scathing article about the crash. It cast aspersions on Conway's ability as a pilot, noting that he had failed three tests early in his career, and it stated that fully half of the working hours of an inspector in Miami was taken up with just monitoring Imperial Airlines and their problems with hydraulic leakage, faulty fuel indicators, bald landing gear tires and fuel seepage from the wing. The Federal Aviation Administration said that the flight crew couldn't know the condition of their aircraft because the logbooks were not kept up to date. "But perhaps the strangest evidence of all," noted TIME, was that Imperial Airline's Chief Flight Engineer John Mayfield repaired a fuel pump motor in the Constellation with a part taken from a 1954 Mercury automobile generator.[387] This jerry-rigging of such a critical part of the airplane was confirmed in public testimony by William Poythress.[388]

The subject of the crossflow valve, the confusion surrounding its position and the inability of the crew to properly deal with the fuel situation were items of much attention by the CAB report when it came out. Flight Engineer Poythress's inability to restart the two fuel-starved engines "indicate the lack of knowledge and inability to diagnose the results of the inoperative fuel boost pump and determine appropriate corrective action." Had Poythress known what he was doing, the two dead engines could have been restarted, and with their power, the plane probably would have made a safe landing.[389] The whole sad story seemed oddly reminiscent of the crash of a DC-3 in 1946, near Byrd Airport and not far from where the Imperial Airlines plane went down. The cause of both nonsked crashes was a deadly mixture of air crew incompetence and poor fuel management.

The Civil Aeronautics Board described the flight crew problems on Flight 201/8: "Confusion prevailed in the cockpit due to lack of coordination and issuing of conflicting orders." Greenlee abruptly claimed control of the airplane and switched from one runway to another, making the fatal loop away from the airport and out into the darkness of the pine forest below. The crew's ignorance of an emergency procedure to drop the landing gear meant loss of precious time, and without the landing gear in position, the attempt to land on the

Still in hospital pajamas, pilot Ronald Conway explains to the press how Imperial Airlines Flight 201/8 crashed in the woods outside Richmond. *Author's collection.*

runway Greenlee indicated was aborted. By then, the plane was needlessly operating on one engine, and its fate and the fates of seventy-seven people on board were sealed.[390] The CAB report also noted the lack of preparation for evacuation and estimated that between thirty seconds and two minutes of time was available for the passengers to get out of the burning plane. At least some of the soldiers would have been able to escape had they known what to do.[391]

The CAB report also condemned Imperial Airlines for shoddy maintenance and management that verged on criminal. However, despite the poor condition of the airplane itself, the investigators concluded that the reason Flight 201/8 crashed lay solely with the actions of the flight crew. "The probable cause of this accident was the lack of coordination and decision, lack of judgement, and lack of knowledge of the equipment resulting in loss of power to three engines creating an emergency situation the crew couldn't handle."[392]

Headlines all over the country trumpeted the gross stupidity of the waste of so many young lives. In Wilkes-Barre, Pennsylvania, the *Evening News* reported that a House Armed Services special committee found "uncertainty and indecision" of regulation of the nonsked industry under the blunt headline "FAA Should Not Have Allowed Plane Flight."[393] James Van Zant, a representative from Pennsylvania, demanded Attorney General

RICHMOND MURDER & MAYHEM

Robert Kennedy investigate the possibility of bringing criminal charges against Imperial Airlines.[394] In Passaic, New Jersey, which had just passed a bleak Christmas, the local newspaper reported the dreadful news of the CAB report. "It is inconceivable to the average person a company engaged in air transport would allow an airplane to leave the ground in charge of an incompetent crew....There seems to ample evidence that officials of Imperials Airlines, owners of the plane, were guilty of criminal neglect. They should be prosecuted."[395]

In Richmond, one headline couldn't have been blunter: "Crash Here Is Blamed on Crew." At the end of this article condemning the incompetence of the flight crew of 201/8 was the reaction of Ronald Conway, still recuperating from the crash in his home in Hollywood, Florida. Commenting on the CAB report, Conway remarked, "It seems kind of ridiculous for them to say the crew didn't know where the cross over valve was. Anyone who flew the plane would have known. It [the valve] was actuated and deactuated a couple times." Looking back on the experience of the crash and the loss of so many lives, Conway lamely concluded, "I really don't know myself what happened there."[396]

In March 1962, Ronald Conway was disciplined by the FAA because of his role in the crash of the Imperial Airlines plane in Richmond and reduced in rank from pilot to copilot, meaning he could no longer command aircraft.[397] He immediately appealed the decision, blaming the crash on his fellow pilot James Greenlee. Greenlee assumed control of the airplane, Conway said, but he admitted that he himself was sitting in the left seat in the cockpit and therefore recognized by the crew as the pilot in command.[398] Conway eventually regained his pilot's status and his reputation. His obituary noted, "Ron flew all over the world with National and Pam Am and ended his career in 1992 with United, flying his favorite 747 from New York to Tokyo." Ronald Conway died in 2013 at the age of eighty-one.[399]

In the wake of the CAB report, William Poythress was stripped of his license by the FAA, not only citing his knowledge of the automobile part being used in the fuel pump but also charging that the former flight engineer knew of a malfunctioning fuel pump the previous day but did not report the problem.[400] Poythress stayed in the aviation business, but not in the air. His obituary noted that he was foreman for Eastern Airlines for many years. Like Conway, he died in 2013 at the age of eighty-one.[401]

In the years that followed the crash of the Imperial Airlines plane, the nonskeds faced the wrath of federal regulations. Twenty carriers went out of business, and the rest were forced to adhere to new and tougher inspections and regulations. By 1967, the surviving nonskeds had rechristened themselves as "supplemental" airlines, becoming a lucrative part of the aviation industry. Fully two-thirds of their business was their old moneymaker, flying for the U.S. military, and business was good in a decade that saw the expansion of the Vietnam War. As to the standards and procedures of the now renamed nonskeds, "all the nuts and kooks have been weeded out," assured Roy Foulke, spokesman for the supplemental airline industry. "We've got a hard-corps [sic] group of operators now."[402]

One victim of the crash of Imperial 201/8 who was a Virginian was Robert Poole, who lived in Front Royal but was among the inductees photographed before boarding the airplane in New Jersey. Poole married when he was twenty and his bride was eighteen, but by 1961, the young couple had separated and their son, Rex, was living with his grandparents. The story of Poole's young son is illustrative of the rippling effects such a loss of life has on individuals and their fates. "I was not quite five years old on the date of the crash, but I still have some very vivid memories," recalled Rex Poole of the traumatic events that shaped his life so long ago. "I remember the day when many people came by to visit, although I didn't realize why at the time. They were coming by to pay their respects. My grandfather took me for a ride in the car on that same day and explained to me that my dad had died in the plane crash." He described his grandmother as never having recovered from the loss of her son.

After the deaths of his grandparents, Poole was forced to go live with the family of an uncle, and once more his life was uprooted. "I frequently find myself imagining how different life would have been if my father had not died in that crash," mused Poole, now sixty-five years old. "I resent the fact that my children never had the opportunity to know him. I also resent the fact that my father, as well as all the other victims, may have died because the government was trying to save a few bucks."[403] The week after his son's death, Rex Poole's grandfather dutifully applied for a GI tombstone.[404] Robert Poole is buried at Front Royal under that marker, with its inscription proudly proclaiming, "PVT US ARMY."

For years, the loss of Imperial Airlines 201/8 was most acutely felt in the little towns where so many of the recruits lived. Memorials were erected in Bethlehem, Pennsylvania, to the fourteen young men lost, and Passaic, New Jersey, created a memorial to its fifteen dead. But in Richmond, the unwilling host to such a tragedy, there was no memorial and no commemoration. Logically, a Virginia State Historic Marker to preserve the memory of the many young men who were lost should have joined the others that dot the

SA 117
IMPERIAL AIRLINES
FLIGHT 201/8

Imperial Airlines Flight 201/8, carrying 74 U.S. Army recruits to Columbia, SC, crashed southeast of Richmond on 8 Nov. 1961. All of the recruits and three of five crew members perished. At the time, the crash was the worst in Virginia history and the second-deadliest in U.S. history for a single civilian aircraft. At fault were poor airline management, substandard maintenance, and crew error. The tragedy resulted in an investigation of the charter aircraft industry that revealed many violations of safety standards. In 1962 Congress mandated that all supplemental carriers reapply for certification by the Civil Aeronautics Board and meet stricter insurance and financial requirements.

DEPARTMENT OF HISTORIC RESOURCES, 2017

A Virginia State Historical Marker, located in a corner of downtown Richmond, commemorates the loss of Imperial Airlines 201/8. *Author's collection.*

perimeter of Richmond International Airport, marking the engagements of the Civil War that took place near there. Perhaps the owner of the facility, the Capital Region Airport Commission, frowned at the idea of a marker commemorating an airplane crash in full view of motorists on their way to meet their plane.

After some years of promoting the idea, family members of some of the young men who died in the Imperial Airlines crash came together and began a letter-writing campaign to prominent officials and politicians, few of whom expressed interest. Ironically, it was only the officials at the recruits' destination that night in 1961 that responded, and the major general in command remembered the recruits who perished during his Veterans Day remarks in Richmond that year. In the end, it was the families and friends of the recruits who applied to the Virginia Department of Historic Resources for a historical marker, and it was the families of the dead who paid the $1,500 for fabricating the marker, which was erected in 2017:

Imperial Airlines Flight 201/8

Imperial Airlines Flight 201/8, carrying 74 U.S. Army recruits to Columbia, SC, crashed southeast of Richmond on 8 Nov. 1961. All of the recruits and three of five crew members perished. At the time, the crash was the worst in Virginia history and the second deadliest in U.S. history for a single civilian aircraft. At fault were poor airline management, substandard maintenance, and crew error. The tragedy resulted in an investigation of the charter aircraft industry that revealed many violations of safety standards. In 1962 Congress mandated that all supplemental carriers reapply for certification by the Civil Aeronautics Board and meet stricter insurance and financial requirements.

The place chosen for the marker is noteworthy. It is near but not on the grounds of the Virginia War Memorial in Richmond, the place where the Commonwealth remembers its fallen service members of many wars. The marker is not even near the War Memorial itself, but instead is down the hill from it, by itself on a corner of South Second Street and Spring Street. Beyond the marker, in this quiet part of Richmond, a vast, empty expanse of grass stretches away into the distance—a featureless vista emblematic of lives cut short and the abridgement of dreams.

NOTES

Chapter 1

1. Commonwealth of Virginia, Bureau of Vital Statistics, State Board of Health, File No. 29420, Alice M. Johnson, October 15, 1917.
2. *The X-Ray, 1917* (Richmond, VA: Students of the Medical College of Virginia, 1917), 43.
3. "Acquit Dr. Johnson," *Alexandria (VA) Gazette*, May 29, 1918, 3.
4. "Denies He Confessed," *Alexandria (VA) Gazette*, May 23, 1918, 2.
5. "Dentist Puts Sole Blame for Secrecy on Dead Girl," *Washington Times*, December 25, 1917, 1.
6. "Accused Dentist May Testify Today," *News and Observer* (Raleigh, NC), May 22, 1918, 1.
7. "Thermometer Drops," *Richmond Times-Dispatch*, December 15, 1917, 2.
8. "Johnson Testifies," *Alexandria (VA) Gazette*, May 25, 1918, 1.
9. "Dr. Johnson Is Held for the Grand Jury," *Richmond Times-Dispatch*, January 12, 1918, 10.
10. "Poison in Stomach," *Alexandria (VA) Gazette*, May 18, 1918, 2.
11. "Death of Dentist's Wife Shrouded in Mystery," *Richmond Times-Dispatch*, December 20, 1917, 5.
12. "Parents of Dead Bride Confer with Detectives," *Richmond Times-Dispatch*, December 27, 1917, 5.
13. "Dr. Johnson Is Held for the Grand Jury," 10.

14. "Keep State from Proving Motive," *Richmond Times-Dispatch*, May 19, 1918, 1.

15. "Charged with Wife Murder," *Alexandria (VA) Gazette*, December 24, 1917, 3.

16. "Johnson Brought Here for Trial," *Richmond Times-Dispatch*, December 24, 1917, 1.

17. Ibid.

18. Ibid.

19. "Johnson Denies Guilt; Asks for Fair Trial," *Richmond Times-Dispatch*, December 25, 1917, 1.

20. Ibid.

21. Ibid.

22. Ibid.

23. "Question of Dr. Johnson's Sanity," *News and Observer* (Raleigh, NC), December 26, 1917, 3.

24. "Miss White Tells of Her Engagement to Dentist," *Richmond Times-Dispatch*, January 20, 1918, 1.

25. "Tiny Blood Clot and Speck of Flesh Figure in Trial," *Richmond Times-Dispatch*, January 3, 1918, 1.

26. Certificate of Death, Commonwealth of Virginia, Bureau of Vital Statistics, State Board of Health, File No. 29420, Alice M. Johnson, December 16, 1917.

27. "Case of Virginia Dentist," *Alexandria (VA) Gazette*, December 27, 1917, 2. The Cluverius case, the Beattie murder and the national attention they both received were explored in Michael Ayres Trotti, *The Body in the Reservoir* (Chapel Hill: University of North Carolina Press, 2008).

28. "New Witness in Johnson Trial," *Richmond Times-Dispatch*, May 17, 1918, 1.

29. "Keep State from Proving Motive," 1.

30. Ibid.

31. Ibid.

32. "Johnson Denies Guilt; Asks for Fair Trial," 1.

33. "Ollie White Letters Are Read to Jury," *Richmond Times-Dispatch*, May 21, 1918, 12.

34. "Denies He Confessed," 2.

35. "Dr. Johnson Is Held for the Grand Jury," *Richmond Times-Dispatch*, January 12, 1918, 10.

36. "Wrote Sweetheart on Day of Marriage," *Richmond Times-Dispatch*, May 23, 1918, 1.

37. Ibid.

38. "Girl Friend Tells of Mrs. Johnson's Death," *Richmond Times-Dispatch*, May 18, 1918, 1.

39. "Ollie White Letters Are Read to Jury," *Richmond Times-Dispatch*, May 21, 1918, 12.

40. "Wrote Sweetheart Day of Marriage," *Richmond Times-Dispatch*, May 23, 1918, 1.

41. "Denies He Confessed," 2.

42. "Evidence Closes in Johnson Case," *Richmond Times-Dispatch*, May 28, 1918, 1.

43. "Johnson Tells Jury of Life Story," *Richmond Times-Dispatch*, May 25, 1918, 1.

44. "Johnson Closely Cross-Questioned," *Richmond Times-Dispatch*, May 26, 1918, 1.

45. Ibid.

46. "Johnson Freed of Wife Murder by Jury," *Richmond Times-Dispatch*, May 29, 1918, 1.

47. Ibid.

48. "Dr. Lemuel Johnson Is Ill at Richmond," *News and Observer* (Raleigh, NC), June 1, 1918, 1.

49. North Carolina State Board of Health, Office of Vital Statistics, Certificate of Death, File No. 18972, Ollie W. Pierce, May 13, 1969.

50. State of North Carolina, Office of Registrar of Deeds, Marriage License, Dr. L.J. Johnson and Lena Snell, December 5, 1924.

51. "Dr. L.J. Johnson Kills Himself," *Richmond Times-Dispatch*, November 18, 1925, 1.

52. North Carolina State Board of Health, Bureau of Vital Statistics, Standard Certificate of Death, No. 453, Lemuel J. Johnson, November 18, 1925.

Chapter 2

53. R.R. Nuckols, *A History of the Government of the City of Richmond, Virginia, and a Sketch of Those Who Administer Its Affairs* (Richmond, VA: Williams Printing Company, 1899), 16.

54. "Dies of His Wounds," *Richmond Dispatch*, January 28, 1896, 1.

55. "His Condition Hopeful," *Richmond Dispatch*, January 11, 1896, 3.

56. "Mr. Shield Is Improving," *Richmond Dispatch*, January 12, 1896, 1.

57. "Col. Winstead's Death," *Western Sentinel* (Winston-Salem, NC), August 30, 1894, 1.

58. "Jumped from the Tower," *Richmond Dispatch*, August 24, 1894, 5.

59. Ibid.

60. Interestingly, the modern Richmond City Hall, whose entire top floor is an observation deck, continues the tradition of providing a space devoted to taking in a view of the city.

61. "Jumped from the Tower," 5.

62. Ibid.

63. Ibid.

64. "City Hall News," *Richmond Dispatch*, August 25, 1894, 4.

65. "Jumped from the Tower," 5.

66. Ibid.

67. "The Tower's Victim," *Richmond Dispatch*, August 24, 1894, 1.

68. "Col. Winstead Buried," *News and Observer* (Raleigh, NC), August 25, 1894, 1.

69. "Col. Winstead's Death," 1.

70. "A Leap to Death," *Atlanta Constitution*, August 24, 1894, 1.

71. "Virginia Affairs," *Baltimore Sun*, August 24, 1894, 2.

72. "Leaped from a Tower," *San Francisco Chronicle*, August 24, 1894, 4.

73. "The Tower's Victim," 1.

74. "Editorial Opinion," *Richmond Planet*, September 1, 1894, 2.

75. "Hints to Suicides," *Richmond Dispatch*, July 15, 1894, 1.

76. Ibid.

77. "Col. Winstead's Death," *Greensboro Patriot*, August 29, 1894, 3.

78. "A Leap to His Death," August 30, 1894, 1.

79. "The Tower's Victim," 1.

80. "Col. Winstead Buried," 1.

Chapter 3

81. "Now Ready for Patients at Westhampton Hospital," *Richmond Times-Dispatch*, July 11, 1918, 5.

82. "500 Wounded Arrive at Westhampton Hospital," *Richmond Times-Dispatch*, December 21, 1918, 1.

83. "Dr. W.A. Hadley Now Occupies Famous Cell in Henrico Prison," *Richmond Times-Dispatch*, September 9, 1921, 12.

84. Ibid.

85. "Abandon Hospital at Westhampton," *Richmond Times-Dispatch*, March 14, 1919, 1.

86. "Alleged Confession of Hadley Placed on Record After Clash," *Richmond Times-Dispatch*, October 26, 1921, 1.

87. "Army Nurse to Assist in Hadley's Capture," *Richmond Times-Dispatch*, January 29, 1919, 1.

88. "Arrest of Husband of Murder Victim Sought by Police," *Richmond Times-Dispatch*, January 24, 1919, 1.

89. "Dr. Hadley, Accused of Wife-Murder, Is Arrested," September 2, 1921, 1.

90. "Alleged Confession of Hadley," 1.

91. "Arrest of Husband of Murder Victim Sought by Police," 1.

92. Ibid.

93. "Police Believe Hadley Killed Wife to Marry Pretty Hospital Nurse," *Richmond Times-Dispatch*, January 28, 1919, 1.

94. "Body of Woman, Believed Slain, Is Found in River," *Richmond Times-Dispatch*, December 31, 1918, 1.

95. Ibid.

96. "Woman's Identity Is Still Mystery," *Richmond Times-Dispatch*, January 1, 1919, 1.

97. Ibid.

98. "Cause of Woman's Death Unrevealed," *Richmond Times-Dispatch*, January 2, 1919, 1.

99. "Body of Woman, Believed Slain," 1.

100. "Deaths," *Cincinnati Enquirer*, December 10, 1918, 7.

101. "Sister-in-Law Told Wife Died in Porto Rico," *Washington Times*, September 18, 1921, 3.

102. "Mrs. Hadley Victim of Disease in Porto Rico on Nov. 24 Wrote Husband," *Richmond Times-Dispatch*, January 25, 1919, 1.

103. "Alleged Confession of Hadley," 1.

104. "Mrs. Hadley Victim of Disease," 1.

105. Ibid.

106. "Army Nurse to Assist in Hadley's Capture," 1.

107. "Identify Murdered Woman as Wife of Army Surgeon," *Paris (TX) Morning News*, January 29, 1919, 2.

108. "Two Hadleys Arrested," *Corpus Christi (TX) Caller-Times*, January 28, 1919, 2.

109. "May Put Pinkertons on Dr. Hadley's Trail," *Evening Sun* (Baltimore, Maryland), February 3, 1919, 2.

110. Ibid.

111. "Officials Awaiting Hadley's Arrest," *Richmond Times-Dispatch*, February 1, 1919, 1.

112. "Corpse of Mrs. Hadley Still Held at Morgue," *Richmond Times-Dispatch*, August 18, 1919, 10.

113. "U.S. General Calls for Federal Troops in W. Va.," *Richmond Times-Dispatch*, September 2, 1921, 1.
114. "Dr. Hadley, Accused of Wife-Murder," 1.
115. Ibid.
116. Ibid.
117. "Hadley Is Speeded to Richmond; Will Arrive Tomorrow," *Richmond Times-Dispatch*, September 7, 1921, 1.
118. "Richmond Widow May Go on Stand at Hadley Trial," *Richmond Times-Dispatch*, September 4, 1921, 1.
119. "Former U.S. Army Surgeon Also Confesses to Murder of a Dr. Griffith, Report," *Richmond Times-Dispatch*, September 6, 1921, 1.
120. "Dr. W.A. Hadley Arrives Here This Morning at 7:10," *Richmond Times-Dispatch*, September 8, 1921, 1.
121. "Dr. Hadley, Accused of Wife-Murder," 1.
122. "Alleged Confession by Hadley Placed on Record After Clash," *Richmond Times-Dispatch*, October 26, 1921, 1.
123. "Hadley Is Speeded to Richmond," 1.
124. "Alleged Confession by Hadley Placed on Record After Clash," 1.
125. "Hadley Is Speeded to Richmond," 1.
126. Ibid.
127. "Dr. J.A. Griffith in France When Mrs. Hadley Was Slain, He Says in Wire to Sherriff Sydnor," *Richmond Times-Dispatch*, September 12, 1921, 1.
128. Ibid.
129. "Hadley to Plead Guilty Is Belief of Officials," *Richmond Times-Dispatch*, September 15, 1921, 1.
130. Ibid.
131. Ibid.
132. "Indict Dr. W.A. Hadley on Wife Murder Charge," *Richmond Times-Dispatch*, October 4, 1921, 1.
133. "Alleged Confession by Hadley Placed on Record After Clash," 1.
134. "Will Lose No Time in Bringing Hadley Back," *Richmond Times-Dispatch*, September 3, 1921, 1.
135. "Alleged Confession by Hadley Placed on Record After Clash," 1.
136. Ibid.
137. Ibid.
138. Ibid.
139. Ibid.
140. "Hadley Found Guilty; Death Penalty Is Fixed," *Richmond Times-Dispatch*, October 27, 1921, 1.

141. Ibid.

142. "Dr. Hadley Dies Today for Murder of His Wife," *Richmond Times-Dispatch*, December 9, 1921, 1.

143. "Dr. Hadley Pays Extreme Penalty Unflinchingly," *Richmond Times-Dispatch*, December 9, 1921, 1.

144. Hollywood Cemetery Company, Ledger, Section L, Lot 23, Society of Friends. The plot map shows five unmarked graves in the plot, interred from 1915 to 1986, aside from Hadley's marked grave.

Chapter 4

145. "To Use Movietone in Local Theater," *Richmond Times-Dispatch*, October 29, 1927, 1.

146. "Richmond Resurgent," *Richmond Times-Dispatch*, June 27, 1926, 6.

147. "Wendenberg Asks Faison Mistrial, Alleging Court Biased," *Richmond Times-Dispatch*, December 17, 1927, 1.

148. Ibid.

149. "Girl Says She Heard Faison Cry Out Guilt After Pistol Shot," *Richmond Times-Dispatch*, December 15, 1927, 1.

150. "Expect Faison Jury to Announce Verdict Soon in Slaying Case," *Richmond Times-Dispatch*, March 19, 1928, 1.

151. "Mrs. Snipes' Death Is Graphically Told by Alleged Slayer," *Daily Press* (Newport News, VA), March 18, 1928, 1.

152. "Faison Case Will Go to Jury Monday; An Early Verdict Seen," *Richmond Times-Dispatch*, March 18, 1928, 1.

153. "Self-Sacrifice Seen as Fatal Shooting Cause," *Richmond Times-Dispatch*, November 17, 1927, 1.

154. "Girl Says She Heard Faison Cry Out," 1.

155. Ibid.

156. Ibid.

157. "Mrs. Snipes' Death Is Graphically Told," 1.

158. "Faison Jurors Deliberate 36 Minutes without a Verdict," *Richmond Times-Dispatch*, December 18, 1927, 1.

159. "Girl Says She Heard Faison Cry Out," 1.

160. "State Rests Its Case Early in Afternoon; Defense Begins," *Richmond Times-Dispatch*, December 16, 1927, 8.

161. Commonwealth of Virginia, Bureau of Vital Statistics, State Board of Health, Death Certificate No. 24616, Elsie Holt Snipes, November 17, 1927.

162. "Faison Is Arrested on Murder Charge in Death of Mrs. Snipes," *Richmond Times-Dispatch*, November 21, 1927, 1.

163. "Man Is Held in Death of Sweetheart," *Clinton (IL) Daily Journal and Public*, December 16, 1927, 1.

164. "Murdered Woman's Diary Indicts Many," *Daily Worker* (Chicago, Illinois), December 16, 1927, 2.

165. "Mrs. Snipes' Diary Looms as a Ghost," *Richmond Times-Dispatch*, December 13, 1927, 1.

166. "Mrs. Faison Raises $1400 for Defense," *Richmond Times-Dispatch*, December 12, 1927, 1.

167. "Mrs. Snipes' Diary Looms as a Ghost," 1.

168. "Human Interest Abounds in Hustings Court Drama," *Richmond Times-Dispatch*, December 14, 1927, 2.

169. "Girl Says She Heard Faison Cry Out," 1.

170. Ibid.

171. Ibid.

172. "Faison Is Arrested on Murder Charge," 1.

173. "Faison Jurors Deliberate 36 Minutes," 1.

174. Ibid.

175. "Faison Breaks Silence; Tells of Fatal Night," *Richmond Times-Dispatch*, November 19, 1927, 1.

176. "Faison Jurors Deliberate 36 Minutes," 1.

177. "Will Set Jan. 4 as New Trial of Faison," *Richmond Times-Dispatch*, December 21, 1927, 1.

178. "Mrs. Snipes' Death Is Graphically Told," 1.

179. "Jury in Faison Case Unable to Return Verdict," *Richmond Times-Dispatch*, March 20, 1928, 1.

180. "Expect Faison Jury to Announce Verdict Soon," 1.

181. "John Wesley Faison Gets One Year for Mrs. Snipes' Death," *Richmond Times-Dispatch*, March 21, 1928, 1.

182. Ibid.

183. "Faison Still Declares Innocence of Killing," *Richmond Times-Dispatch*, March 22, 1928, 1.

184. "John Wesley Faison Gets One Year," 1.

185. "Crime and Punishment," *Richmond Times-Dispatch*, March 21, 1928, 6.

186. Ibid.

187. "Agrees with Editor on Crime Beliefs," *Richmond Times-Dispatch*, letters to editor, April 2, 1928, 6.

188. "Faison Still Maintains Innocence and Resolves to Lead Higher Life," *Richmond Times-Dispatch*, 1.

189. "John Wesley Faison Begins Serving Prison Term," *Richmond Times-Dispatch*, April 1, 1928, 2.

190. "Faison Leaves Prison; Is Greeted by Infant," *Richmond Times-Dispatch*, October 30, 1928, 15.

191. "John W. Faison" (obituary), *Daily Times* (Salisbury, MD), February 13, 1972.

192. "Martha B. Faison" (obituary), *Daily Times* (Salisbury, MD), January 31, 1984.

Chapter 5

193. VCU Libraries, "History of Richmond Professional Institute," https://guides.library.vcu.edu/c.php?g=47717&p=298451.

194. "RPI Student Shot, Killed; Former Roommate Held," *Richmond Times-Dispatch*, May 8, 1956, 1.

195. Ibid.

196. "Accused Slayer Says He Planned Suicide," *Progress-Index* (Petersburg, VA), May 9, 1956, 1.

197. *Ripples*, Bridgewater College yearbook, 1955, 51.

198. "RPI Student Shot, Killed," 1.

199. "Ex-Roommate Held in Death of RPI Student," *Daily Press* (Newport News, VA), May 8, 1956, 1.

200. "'I Wish I Could Cry' Says Student's Slayer," *Richmond News Leader*, May 9, 1956, 1.

201. "RPI Officials Told Vischio Had Pistol," *Richmond Times-Dispatch*, May 9, 1956, 1.

202. Ibid.

203. "RPI Student Shot, Killed," 1.

204. "RPI Officials Told Vischio Had Pistol," 1.

205. "Vischio Never Fired Pistol Before," *Richmond Times-Dispatch*, May 10, 1956, 3.

206. Ibid.

207. "RPI Student Shot, Killed," 1.

208. Ibid.

209. Ibid.

210. "College Student Shot to Death by Ex-Roommate," *Boston Globe*, May 8, 1956, 15.

211. "I Wish I Could Cry," 1.

212. "Accused Slayer Says He Planned Suicide," 1.

213. "I Wish I Could Cry," 1.

214. "Vischio Never Fired Pistol Before," 3.

215. "I Wish I Could Cry," 1.

216. "Provost Declines to Comment on RPI Investigation Move," *Richmond News Leader*, May 12, 1956, 2.

217. "Ex-RPI Student Is Indicted in Slaying of Roommate," *Richmond News Leader*, June 4, 1956, 23.

218. "Vischio Gets Life Term in RPI Student's Slaying," *Richmond News Leader*, January 2, 1957, 1.

219. "RPI Slaying Suspect Sent Ordered to Hospital for Observation," *Richmond News Leader*, June 11, 1956, 25.

220. "Vischio Trial Set for November 27," *Richmond News Leader*, November 7, 1956, 8.

221. "RPI Shooting Case Opens Tomorrow," *Richmond News Leader*, January 1, 1957, 19.

222. "Vischio Gets Life Term in RPI Student's Slaying," 1.

223. "RPI Staff Increases Sought," *Richmond News Leader*, March 8, 1957, 4.

224. "Student Criticism High Due to Committee Action," *Prescript*, May 17, 1956, 2.

225. Ibid.

226. "RPI Is a Help Where It Is," *Richmond News Leader*, July 30, 1957, 10.

227. "Vischio, Alfred" (obituary), *Boston Globe*, August 30, 2007, 33.

Chapter 6

228. "Officer Dies in Gun Fight with Thug," *Richmond Times-Dispatch*, February 5, 1937, 1.

229. "Filling Station Here Entered by Burglars," *Richmond Times-Dispatch*, August 12, 1935, 16.

230. "Police Press Search in $1,100 Theft Here," *Richmond Times-Dispatch*, May 8, 1936, 24.

231. "Linden Street Fire Causes Traffic Jam," *Richmond Times-Dispatch*, April 19, 1938, 4.

232. "Police Hunting Slayers of 2 on Slim Clues," *Richmond News Leader*, October 21, 1940, 1.
233. Ibid.
234. "Lee Now," *Richmond Times-Dispatch*, October 20, 1940, 11.
235. "Police Hunting Slayers of 2 on Slim Clues," 1.
236. Ibid.
237. "Negro Youth Arrested in Murder of Grocer, Tibbs' Slayers Hunted," *Richmond Times-Dispatch*, October 22, 1940, 1.
238. "Tibbs, Police Veteran, Slain, Killer Escapes; Grocer, 72, Murdered," *Richmond Times-Dispatch*, October 21, 1940, 1.
239. Ibid.
240. Jenny Van Volkum (daughter of Officer Tibbs) and Jody Kerns (Tibbs's granddaughter), personal interview, November 8, 2012.
241. "3 Veteran Police Officers Are Dismissed 'For the Good of the Service,'" *Richmond Times-Dispatch*, October 22, 1940, 1.
242. Ibid.
243. "Tibbs Buried as Officers Offer Tribute," *Richmond Times-Dispatch*, October 23, 1940, 5.
244. "Richmond Sideshow," *Richmond News Leader*, October 25, 1940, 11.
245. "Pay Safety Men More and Have More Men," *Richmond News Leader*, August 20, 1941, 6.
246. "Tickets Go on Sale for Tibbs' Benefit," *Richmond Times-Dispatch*, October 31, 1940, 5.
247. "Tibbs Widow Is Allotted Fund by the City," *Richmond Times-Dispatch*, March 25, 1942, 7.
248. "In Memorandum, Tibbs," *Richmond News Leader*, October 20, 1945, 13.
249. Van Volkum and Kerns, interview, November 8, 2012.
250. Ibid.
251. Ibid.
252. "Family Honors Police Officer Killed in 1940," *Richmond Times-Dispatch*, May 16, 2012, 5.
253. In 2012, I was invited to review the Tibbs file at the Richmond Police Department, with the condition that I could not copy any of the information, as it was considered an "open case." A Richmond detective who was assisting me held up the photo of Tibbs's body, said, "What do you see wrong with this picture?" and pointed out the one empty cartridge loop on his belt.
254. "Family Honors Police Officer Killed," 5.

255. Ibid.

256. Ibid.

257. Letter, via e-mail, William K. Shipman, Associate General Counsel, City of Richmond Police Department, to Selden Richardson, August 27, 2020.

258. Van Volkum and Kerns, interview, November 8, 2012.

Chapter 7

259. "Census Takers Are Prying Loose Much Information," *Richmond Times-Dispatch*, January 5, 1920, 1.

260. Department of Commerce, Bureau of the Census, Fourteenth Census of the United States: 1920—Population, Richmond City, Madison Ward, 2,899.

261. *Richmond, Virginia, Register of Marriages in the Year Ending 31st December 1930*, 36. Although her husband's name was "Merriman," even Violet seems to have used that spelling interchangeably with "Merryman." Since she appeared in the press as "Merryman," that is the preferred spelling for purposes of this account.

262. Violet Merryman, "I Turned in My Lover for Murder," *Actual Detective Stories of Women in Crime* (January 1938): 21.

263. Ibid.

264. "Murder Mystery Chronology," *Richmond News Leader*, April 13, 1937, 10.

265. "Family Sees Skull, Bones as Hawkins'," *Richmond Times-Dispatch*, 1.

266. Merryman, "I Turned in My Lover for Murder," 21.

267. "Judge Expected to Set Trial Date in Murder Cases; Violet Merryman Confesses," *Richmond Times-Dispatch*, August 4, 1942, 4.

268. "'I Loved Ed Like Brother,' 'Captain' Says," *Richmond Times-Dispatch*, March 9, 1937, 1.

269. "Howard Guilty, Gets Life Term for Murder," *Richmond Times-Dispatch*, April 16, 1937, 1.

270. Merryman, "I Turned in My Lover for Murder," 21.

271. "Family Sees Skull, Bones," 1.

272. Merryman, "I Turned in My Lover for Murder," 21.

273. Ibid.

274. "Hawkins Slaying Reported Solved," *Bristol (TN) Herald Courier*, March 10, 1937, 7.

275. "I Loved Ed Like Brother," 1.

276. "Mrs. Rebecca F. Berry" (obituary), *Richmond News Leader*, January 11, 1937, 23.

277. "Murder Mystery Chronology," 10.

278. "'The Captain' Is Ordered to Jail as a Vagrant," *Richmond Times-Dispatch*, March 3, 1937, 4.

279. "Family Sees Skull, Bones," 1.

280. Ibid.

281. "Special Panel May Consider 'The Captain,'" *Richmond Times-Dispatch*, March 11, 1937, 1.

282. "Family Sees Skull, Bones," 1.

283. "'Captain' Begs Public to Wait for His Story," *Richmond Times-Dispatch*, March 13, 1937, 1.

284. Ibid.

285. "State Witness," *Richmond News Leader*, April 13, 1937, 10.

286. "Howard Goes with Jury to Crime Scene," *Richmond Times-Dispatch*, April 14, 1937, 1.

287. "Howard Guilty, Gets Life Term," *Richmond Times-Dispatch*, April 16, 1937, 1.

288. "Laban Howard Back at City Jail," *Richmond Times-Dispatch*, April 17, 1937, 4.

289. Merryman, "I Turned in My Lover for Murder," 21.

290. "Violet Denies She Maligned City's Finest," *Richmond Times-Dispatch*, December 1, 1937, 1.

Chapter 8

291. *Richmond News Leader*, July 18, 1942, 4.

292. "Last Night Was Hottest in History of Richmond," *Richmond News Leader*, July 18, 1942, 1.

293. "Increase in Crime Noted in Wake of Intense Heat," *Richmond News Leader*, July 21, 1942, 3.

294. Certificate of Birth, Commonwealth of Virginia, Bureau of Vital Statistics, State Board of Health, File No. 33017, Emma Virginia Dooms, July 16, 1916.

295. Department of Commerce—Bureau of the Census, Fifteenth Census of the United States: 1930, Population Schedule, Enumeration District No. 21-17, April 7, 1930.

1-2

296. "Hustings Court Jury Returns 46 True Bills," *Richmond Times-Dispatch*, November 5, 1935, 11.
297. "2 Woman and a Soldier Team Up in Orgy of Crime," *New York Daily News*, December 27, 1942, 64.
298. "Jury Orders Death of Soldier Held for Man's Murder Here," *Richmond Times-Dispatch*, September 18, 1942, 1.
299. The Abraham Lincoln Brigade Archives, https://alba-valb.org/volunteers/harry-edward-farris.
300. "Jury Orders Death of Soldier," 1.
301. Ibid.
302. "Violet Merryman Found Guilty; Sentence Is Fixed at 25 Years," *Richmond Times-Dispatch*, October 27, 1942, 1.
303. "Jury Orders Death of Soldier," 1.
304. "When Justice Triumphed in Virginia," *Knoxville (TN) Journal*, December 27, 1942, 26.
305. "Two Murders Baffle City, County Police," *Richmond Times-Dispatch*, July 20, 1942, 1.
306. "Hargrove" (obituary), *Richmond Times-Dispatch*, July 20, 1942, 14.
307. "Third Straight Record Falls as Temperature Hits 99 Degrees," *Richmond Times-Dispatch*, July 20, 1942, 1.
308. "Driver of Cab Used by Farris Appears in Court," *Richmond Times-Dispatch*, August 15, 1942, 5.
309. "Police Catch Emma Dooms in Flat Here," *Richmond Times-Dispatch*, August 1, 1942, 1.
310. U.S. Department of Labor, Naturalization Service, Declaration of Intention, No. 1634, Vincio Ernesto Bichi, April 25, 1924.
311. D.D.S. Form 1 [draft card], "Vincio Ernesto Bichi," October 16, 1940.
312. "Jury Orders Death of Soldier," 1.
313. Ibid.
314. "Two Women and Man Sought by Detectives in Murder Case," *Richmond Times-Dispatch*, July 21, 1942, 4.
315. Commonwealth of Virginia, Department of Health, Bureau of Vital Statistics, Certificate of Death, Vinicio Bichi, July 20, 1942, State File No. 15205, Registered No. 1610.
316. "Soldier Used Long Knife in Murders," *Richmond Times-Dispatch*, July 28, 1942, 1.
317. "Police Jail Last of Trio in Slayings," *Richmond Times-Dispatch*, August 3, 1942, 1.
318. Ibid.

319. "Evidence in Knife Slayings," *Richmond Times-Dispatch*, August 1, 1942, 1.

320. "October Area Highlights," *Richmond News Leader*, November 2, 1942, 12.

321. "Girl Who Attracts Murderers Is Mixed Up in More Killings," *New York Daily News*, August 16, 1942, 3.

322. "Police Catch Emma Dooms in Flat Here," 1.

323. "Soldier Used Long Knife in Murders," 1.

324. "Jury Orders Death of Soldier," 1.

325. Ibid.

326. Ibid.

327. "When Justice Triumphed in Virginia," 26.

328. "Jury Orders Death of Soldier," 1.

329. Ibid.

330. Ibid.

331. "When Justice Triumphed in Virginia," 26.

332. Ibid.

333. "Virginia Dooms, Foregoing Jury Trial, Faces Court," *Richmond News Leader*, April 3, 1943, 4.

334. "Woman Gets 30-Year Term for Slaying," *Richmond Times-Dispatch*, April 9, 1943, 10.

335. "Farris Loses Last Chance for His Life," *Richmond Times-Dispatch*, October 3, 1943, 7.

336. "Farris Goes to Death in Chair," *Richmond News Leader*, October 15, 1943, 3.

337. "Emma Dooms Given 20 Years in Bichi Death," *Richmond Times-Dispatch*, October 21, 1943, 6.

338. "2 Woman and a Soldier Team Up," 64.

339. "State Farm for Women Strives for Useful Lives," *Richmond Times-Dispatch*, May 27, 1962, 79.

340. "Mrs. Merryman Testifies Slaying Trial Was Unfair," *Richmond Times-Dispatch*, March 31, 1970, B-1.

341. United States Social Security Applications and Claims Index, 1936–2007, "Emma Virginia Dooms."

342. Ibid.

343. "Woman Held 27 Years Files Writ," *Richmond Times-Dispatch*, November 14, 1969, 35.

344. Ibid.

345. "Prisoner Files Plea in Henrico," *Richmond Times-Dispatch*, January 9, 1970, 21.

346. "Mrs. Merryman Testifies," 33.

347. Ibid.

348. "Merryman Plea for Release Turned Down," *Richmond Times-Dispatch*, April 21, 1970, 19.

349. Commonwealth of Virginia, Department of Health, Division of Vital Records, Certificate of Death, Eades, George Thomas, August 25, 1987, State File No. 87-029166.

350. Commonwealth of Virginia, Department of Public Health—Richmond, Certificate of Death, Eades, Violet Ellen Berry, September 3, 1988, State File No. 88-031338.

Chapter 9

351. "How Safe Are the Nonskeds?," *New York Daily News*, December 17, 1961, 80.

352. "Crash Probers Study Possibility of Hearing," *Richmond News Leader*, July 20, 1951, 1.

353. "Airline Probe Opened Shortly Before Crash," *Progress-Index* (Petersburg, VA), November 12, 1961, 1.

354. "Fiery Plane Crash Kills 77; Most of Them Young Army Draftees," *Kane (PA) Republican*, November 9, 1961, 1.

355. "Traffic Ticket Saves Clifton Youth; Another Joins AF; 'Nice Kids' Perish," *Paterson (NJ) Evening News*, November 9, 1961, 1.

356. "77 Die Here in Worst Va. Air Crash," *Richmond News-Leader*, November 9, 1961, 1.

357. "Conway, Capt. Ronald H." (obituary), *Miami Herald*, December 10, 2013, B-4.

358. The ages and military affiliation of Greenlee and Poythress were taken from photos of their grave markers on the Find A Grave website.

359. *Civil Aeronautics Board—Aircraft Accident Report, Imperial Airlines, Inc., Lockheed Constellation L-049, N2737A, Byrd Field, Richmond, Va.*, November 8, 1961.

360. "The Crash of Flight 201/8," *Virginia Eagles, Official Newsletter of the Virginia Aeronautical Historical Society* 34, no. 1 (January–February–March 2011): 25.

361. *Civil Aeronautics Board—Aircraft Accident Report*, November 8, 1961.

362. "Rust Found in Engines GI Crash Probe Told," *Miami Herald*, November 22, 1961. 55.

363. "74 Deaths Attributed to Errors," *Spokesman-Review* (Spokane, WA), February 7, 1962, 26.

364. "'Impact Didn't Feel Severe,' Pilot Says of Airliner Crash," *Richmond Times Dispatch*, November 11, 1961, 1.

365. Ibid.

366. "77 Die Here in Worst Va. Air Crash," 1.

367. "Desperate Landing Tried, Witness Says," *Richmond News-Leader*, November 9, 1961, 1.

368. "77 Die Here in Worst Va. Air Crash," 1.

369. Ibid.

370. "Clerk Recalls Young Recruits," *Claremore (OK) Daily Progress*, November 9, 1961, 1.

371. Ibid.

372. "Flaming Plane Crash Kills 22 Local Army Recruits," *Herald News* (Passaic, NJ), November 9, 1961, 1.

373. "News of Tragedy Stuns and Embitters Families Only Hours After Farewells," *Herald News* (Passaic, NJ), November 9, 1961, 1.

374. Ibid.

375. "Casualty List in Plane Crash," *Morning Call* (Allentown, PA), November 10, 1961, 16.

376. "Lehigh Valley Is Shocked by Tragic Deaths of 29 Recruits and Draftees in Plane Crash," *Morning Call* (Allentown, PA), November 10, 1961, 1.

377. "Area's First Draftees Since Fatal Air Crash Go by Train," *News* (Paterson, NJ), November 28, 1961, 1.

378. "Plane's Engines to Go to D.C.," *Richmond News Leader*, November 11, 1961, 1.

379. "Intricate Researching Identifies Crash Dead," *Richmond News Leader*, November 13, 1961, 1.

380. "Mary Linda Johns" (obituary), *Tampa Tribune*, November 11, 1961, 26.

381. "Most of Deaths in Plane Crash Are Attributed to Suffocation," *Richmond Times Dispatch*, November 11, 1961, 1.

382. "First of Bodies Reach Ft. Lee," *Richmond Times Dispatch*, November 11, 1961, 6.

383. "Most of Deaths in Plane Crash," 1.

384. "First of Bodies Reach Ft. Lee," 6.

385. "CAB Swiftly Slates Air Crash Hearings," *Richmond News Leader*, November 13, 1961, 1.

386. "McNamara to Tighten Troop Plane Controls," *Richmond News Leader*, November 17, 1961, 1.

387. "Aviation: A Few Discrepancies," *TIME*, December 15, 1961.

388. *Civil Aeronautics Board—Aircraft Accident Report*, November 8, 1961, 13.

389. Ibid., 20.

390. Ibid., 23.

391. Ibid., 23–24.

392. Ibid., 25.

393. "FAA Should Not Have Allowed Plane Flight," *Evening News* (Wilkes-Barre, PA), February 9, 1962, 18.

394. "Asks Study," *Evening News* (Wilkes-Barre, PA), February 9, 1962, 18.

395. "The Appalling Report on Air Tragedy," *Herald-News* (Passaic, NJ), February 7, 1962, 12.

396. "Crash Here Is Blamed on Crew," *Richmond Times Dispatch*, February 7, 1962, 1.

397. "FAA Revokes Licenses of Two," *Pensacola (FL) News Journal*, March 23, 1962, 2.

398. "Death Flight Pilot Says Co-Pilot Held Controls," *Miami News*, April 12, 1962, 47.

399. "Conway, Capt. Ronald H." (obituary), *Miami Herald*, December 10, 2013, B-4.

400. "Loses License in Crash Probe," *Kansas City (MO) Times*, March 21, 1962, 31.

401. "Poythress, William F." (obituary), *Atlanta Journal-Constitution*, March 30, 2013, B-6.

402. "High Flying Supplemental," *TIME* (June 30, 1967): 11.

403. Rex Poole, e-mail message to author, April 27, 2022.

404. Application for Headstone or Marker, Department of Defense Form 1330, "Robert Vernon Poole," November 14, 1961.

ABOUT THE AUTHOR

S elden Richardson is a local historian who writes and lectures about history and architecture in his native city of Richmond, Virginia. He is the author of *Built by Blacks: African American Architecture and Neighborhoods in Richmond, Virginia* (The History Press, 2008) and *The Tri-State Gang in Richmond: Murder and Robbery in the Great Depression* (The History Press, 2012).

Visit us at
www.historypress.com
....